BODY BUILDER'S BIBLE

For Men and Women

VIC BOFF

ARCO PUBLISHING, INC.
NEW YORK

This book is affectionately dedicated to the memory of my parents, Samuel and Rose Boff, for the years of love and sacrifice that made my world of physical culture possible.

Published by Arco Publishing, Inc.
215 Park Avenue South, New York, N.Y. 10003

Library of Congress Cataloging in Publication Data

Boff, Vic.
 Body builder's bible for men and women.

 Includes index.
 1. Bodybuilding.   I. Title.
 GV546.5.B64   1985   646.7′5   85-1444
 ISBN 0-668-05625-8 (Cloth Edition)
 ISBN 0-668-05630-4 (Paper Edition)

Printed in the United States of America

10 9 8 7 6 5 4 3 2 1

Contents

Acknowledgments

With great appreciation I acknowledge the contributions of Anibal Lopez, world-renowned physique champion, and to his daughter, Annette Lopez, for their exercise photographs; their photographer, Denie; models Sirkka-Lisa Carrier and Joe Koytila and photographer Abe Lavalais; the President's Council on Physical Fitness and Sports; David P. Willoughby, famed historian and physical fitness authority; the late George F. Jowett; my dear wife, Ann, who helped with the manuscript; Barbara Settanni, who typed the manuscript; my good friend Jim Sanders, a great artist and illustrator, for his assistance, enthusiasm, and fine illustrations; and to the world-famous York Barbell Company of York, Pennsylvania, and its subsidiaries, Strength and Health Publishing Company, and *Muscular Development* magazine for their generous contribution of information, photographs, and illustrations.

Preface

Here at last is a concise, easy-to-understand, illustrated book on the hows and whys of bodybuilding, presenting different exercise systems designed to help develop your physique and figure to the degree of fitness you desire.

Today, above all else, men and women desire beauty and symmetry of form. If you only realized how easily these physical assets can be acquired and retained, you would gladly devote some time each day to intelligently applied exercises, the only means to their attainment. It is important to understand that "life is motion" and that every vital, living thing demands action, that action demands muscles, and that muscles demand *exercise*. You must follow a progressive, systematic, scientific method of exercising that meets all of your body's needs. The proper method will build and maintain a well-proportioned, fully developed body, giving you strength, stamina, speed, power, and vigor, as well as good posture, balance, and coordination. Remember, the human body increases in efficiency with use and deteriorates with disuse. Lack of activity—the failure to exercise—leads to flabbiness and loss of muscle tone.

Now, more than ever before, home training has become recognized the world over as an excellent way to obtain superior fitness and a superior physique. Although much of the weight-training and fitness equipment used in gyms and spas is excellent for bodybuilders, athletes, and competitive weight lifters, its high cost and size make it impractical for home use. When you feel ready to master complicated movements or skills on apparatus of any sort, or to perform intricate feats, you should attend a properly equipped spa, which has the further advantage of skilled supervision.

If you are the kind of person who has always wanted to be strong and healthy with a fine build or figure but who has put off training and bodybuilding because you could not attend a gym or spa, for whatever reason, you need wait no longer.

The home bodybuilding systems and routines described in this book are fully illustrated and explained in detail, with the necessary apparatus requirements spelled out. The exercises are suitable for both male and female bodybuilders.

The proper mental attitude, intelligently applied exercise, wholesome food, fresh air, bathing, sun baths, relaxation, and sleep, all determined by individual needs, are essential to promote health and strength.

The results you obtain will be governed by the effort you put into your exercises and routines.

1

Your Total Fitness Program

There is no perfect system of exercise. If there were, it would have to suit all ages, purposes, circumstances, and bodily requirements. Its use would result in the highest degree of proper muscular balance and symmetry, speed, strength, and endurance; the utmost coordination between mind and muscle; an aptitude for sports and games; agility and suppleness; and so forth. These attributes cover a range too wide to be achieved by any one individual at any one time.

However, some exercises and systems *are* better than others, they can bring about certain definite results, and their utilization *can* result in one or more of the above-mentioned benefits. For the upper body, you can choose from barbell and dumbbell exercises, chest-expander work, hand balancing, rope climbing, the roman ring, and bar work. The legs could get their share from running, cycling, tumbling, hill climbing, and rope skipping. General and supplemental workouts could include wrestling, swimming, handball, and tennis.

Proper muscle growth depends upon stimulation and upon accumulation of appropriate nutriments to promote healthy development. The longevity and endurance of your body depends upon the condition of your organs. Your body's parts must receive training according to their requirements and the nature of their construction. One method will not do it all. Neither will one set or program of exercises be suitable for every person.

You must work the exercises you choose into a well-planned system, for example, chest-expander work for the upper body and barbell exercises for the lower back and legs, supplemented by rope skipping. Or you might combine barbell and dumbbell exercises with cycling and sprinting. Each system should include exercises to counteract slow muscle-developing movements and exercises that promote balance and suppleness.

Because no two people are alike, each person using the exercises in this book will benefit differently from them. For example, if you are now primarily anxious to build up the size of your muscles, you will find the weight-training program with the barbell and dumbbells to be most effective.

If you are underweight or tend to be thin, you should avoid practicing various athletic sports and games while you are trying to build up your muscles. Beginners often imagine that the more exercise they do, the better and quicker results they will get. This is a big mistake, since nature does not work that way. You must alternate days when you do exercises that gradually require your muscles to overcome strenuous resistance with days of rest, so that nature can repair and build the muscle fibers. If you happen to be devoted to some athletic sport that you cannot give up, then it is best for you to practice muscle-building exercises during the off-season, when you are not practicing that sport.

After you have more fully developed your muscles and attained your optimum weight, you can safely indulge in all the varied forms of athletic activity you desire, as often as you wish. (Of course, if you should happen to be *overweight*, then daily exercise is a necessity.)

Goals

Everyone should be able to take full advantage of these exercise programs, which have been designed so that

- You will know exactly how and where to begin, and what to do every step of the way.
- You will begin easily, without strain or upset, no matter how long it has been since you last engaged in vigorous physical activity.
- You will make steady progress toward a level of fitness that you have determined is most suitable for you, and that you will be able to maintain.
- You will have the satisfaction of being able to measure your progress as you proceed.
- You will be able to work out at home, without (or with a minimum of) special equipment.

How This Book Is Organized

You will "begin at the beginning" in Chapter 2 with a quick explanation of what the muscles are and what they do. If you understand just how your body works, you will better understand how each exercise affects your muscle growth.

Then, in Chapter 3, you will start your conditioning program with a few warm-up exercises. It is important never to begin an exercise program with sudden strenuous activity; this can be very dangerous. Instead, begin each session with a graduated program of exercise, as detailed here.

Now that your body is ready, you can get down to business. In

Chapters 4 and 5, you will be introduced to the basics of weight training—what it's all about, how it can help you, what you will need to know.

If you are now primarily anxious to build up your muscle size, you will find the weight-training program with the barbell and dumbbells in Chapters 6 and 7 most effective. Study these chapters and progressively coordinate the barbell with the dumbbell exercises, along with the bench routines in Chapter 14.

Proper development of the waist or abdominal muscles is of basic importance to everyone's health and strength. It has far-reaching, beneficial effects on the entire body. Chapter 8 shows you how a few minutes a day given to the right kind of exercise can soon transform a bulging waistline into a strong, protective wall of muscle.

The appearance of the whole upper body depends upon the proper symmetry of the neck. Chapter 9 shows you the benefits of neck exercises.

In Chapter 10 you will learn all about the importance of stretching and keeping your muscles limber, something every fitness enthusiast and bodybuilder does conscientiously before and after every workout.

Once you have mastered the exercises laid out in these chapters, you should be conditioned sufficiently to try the advanced weight-training routines in Chapter 11. And those of you especially interested in developing greater strength with weight-lifting techniques will want to try the Olympic weight-lifting movements and routines detailed in Chapter 12.

Since many of you may want to gauge the success of your weight training by measuring your muscles, I have included Chapter 13 to show how to do it and how to accurately record your measurements.

In Chapter 14 you will find exercises and routines with the various types of accessory equipment available to the fitness and weight-training enthusiast. You will be surprised at the variety of relatively inexpensive and useful equipment you can buy to aid in your quest for a healthy and fit body.

To enhance your total shape-up program, to offset strain and cramps, to aid your muscle flexibility and growth, Chapter 15 will teach you all about the secrets of massage.

Finally, in Chapter 16, you will learn how to choose physical activities or sports for recreation, health, fitness, and pleasure.

Diet

Exercise alone does not build muscle. In order to develop your muscles in size and strength, you should eat sufficient amounts of whole food. Three square meals a day are essential, including a generous amount of protein. The best sources of protein are milk, eggs, cheese, meat, fish, and poultry, balanced by proper amounts of whole grains, fresh vegetables, and fruits.

Because many of our fruits, grains, and vegetables come from partially depleted soils, and because of the long time span between the harvesting and the time we set the foods on the table, I highly recommend that a good brand of vitamin-mineral supplement be taken with some regularity. Tobacco, alcohol, hot condiments, and white sugar and flour products are best avoided entirely. You cannot maintain health or improve physically on an inadequate diet. So cut out devitaminized and demineralized foods—which are properly termed "junk foods."

Generally, there are two ways of eating. You can eat to fill your stomach and temporarily appease your hunger and appetite. Almost any food will do this. Or you can eat balanced, natural foods, chosen with the object of satisfying the complete nutritional needs of your body. There is no reason why the second way should not be just as enjoyable as the first, with the added advantage that the real hungers of the blood and body cells for first-class building and servicing materials will be satisfied, as well as the hunger of the stomach.

When the diet is properly balanced to meet the needs of the body for protein, carbohydrates, minerals, and vitamins, perfect performance in building and repair will be taking place throughout its billions of cells, producing needed energy. Each organ will carry on its work normally, and when all the waste products are adequately removed, superb health and vitality will become a reality.

Study as much as you can about nutrition, and you will begin to understand what it is all about—a working knowledge of the functions of vitamins and minerals should become a part of everyone's everyday health information.

If you have a nutritional or other specific problem that you find difficult to overcome, seek the help of a physician who is an expert on nutrition.

2

The Muscles That Make You Tick

Before you begin to develop your physique, improve your health, and increase your strength, vigor, and drive, you should know which muscles make you tick. Should you desire to develop any particular set of muscles to add to the proportions and appearance of your body, you should concentrate on exercises designed to develop those specific muscle groups. Do likewise if any particular sport or specific type of work that you do demands that certain muscles be developed to their maximum efficiency and strength.

The human body contains about 520 muscles, which make up about 40 to 50 percent of the body's weight. There are three types of muscles: the voluntary (striped) muscles, which we can consciously control; the involuntary, or unstriped muscles, which function without our conscious control (such as the muscles that carry food to the stomach); and the heart muscles. In this book, we will be dealing mainly with those voluntary muscles.

Muscles come in various shapes and lengths. Some, like the biceps of the arm, are spindle-shaped, while others, like the sartorious of the thigh, are long and ribbonlike. Some, like the biceps and the frontal thigh muscles, make up the major bulk of their area, while others, such as those of the forearm, the calf, and the back of the thigh, have short "bellies" but long, tendinous connections. Still others, such as those of the anterior wall of the abdomen, form broad, thick sheets. Muscles such as the biceps are only capable of direct, straight movements, while others, such as the latissimus dorsi and trapezius of the back are capable of diversified action.

When a voluntary muscle is ordered by your brain to work (for example, when you want to bend your arm), it contracts, shortening the muscle into a heavier bulk and pulling on surrounding parts of the body. All muscles function by contraction, and each muscle is designed to counterbalance another. For example, the biceps bends the arm, while the triceps straightens it; the muscles on the back of the thigh bend the leg at the knee, while the quadriceps femoris straightens it. These opposing functions help the body to maintain balance and natural position.

Muscles run on sugar supplied from the bloodstream in the form of glycogen. Glycogen is released from the liver into the bloodstream in proportion to physical demand. Just as the combustion of fuel in an engine supplies both energy and heat, the combustion of sugar in a muscle liberates energy and heat. That is one reason why you feel warm after exercising.

As muscle activity takes place, old tissue cells break down and are replaced by new cells. The breakdown rate depends upon the amount of physical exertion inflicted on the muscles. The average person often believes that forcing the muscles to do more work than they are used to will break down more old tissue faster, and thus result in a greater replenishment of new tissue. In fact, this is wrong—too little time elapses between exercise periods for sufficient replenishment to occur, and serious injuries to the muscles can result.

Rhythmic exercise, properly planned, stimulates the muscles and promotes better blood circulation, which washes away the waste products and at the same time conveys the necessary nutrition for the replenishment of the muscular tissue. In this way, proper exercise will build up the muscles and raise your fatigue threshold.

NOTE: Short muscles can stand more direct exercise than can the longer and more complexly arranged muscles. Thus, the muscles of the upper arm, the forearm, and the calves can be employed more vigorously than other muscles without ill effects.

Muscular tissue runs the gamut from atrophied (totally degenerated due to lack of use or disease) to overdeveloped. For most of us, muscles probably range from being too flaccid to being too hard. Flaccidity is caused by insufficient use of the muscles. The tissues are loose or coarsely combined, decreasing the natural power of contraction. Exercise for flaccid muscles should be more graduated than for hard muscles, since they are easily fatigued and more liable to strain.

Even people who are out of shape have some very hard muscles. For example, calf muscles are very often the most used muscles; they lift the body's entire weight with every step. Consequently, the calf muscles are very strong, and strong muscles call for a denser (or hard) formation of tissue. If muscles become too hard, however, excessive exercise is not the remedy. Massage, by relaxing the muscles, can aid in their eventual development.

The object of learning about the muscles of the body in this manner is to know the difference in the type, function, and utility of each muscle. Thus we can exercise the muscles properly. The following is a breakdown of the major voluntary muscles in your body.

Trapezius Muscles

The trapezius muscles are the most versatile in the body. They originate along the spine and branch off, triangular fashion, across the shoulders and up the back of the neck. They aid in back functions such as shrugging the shoulders, holding the shoulders back, and maintaining the erect posture of the head. As these muscles develop, they shorten, pulling back the shoulders more squarely, keeping the back flat and pulling the head back with the chin up. They correct round shoulders, protruding shoulder blades, and the forward sag of the head, giving a correct, erect posture. Good trapezius development is an indication of strength and is seen to advantage in the competitive weight-lifter and athlete.

Deltoid Muscles

The latissimus dorsi and trapezius muscles can be freely exercised without any thought of strain, but not so the deltoid muscles that spread over the shoulders and the upper arm. On the average person they are about the weakest muscles in the body. Because they permit the arm to function in all movements that hold it out level with the shoulders, they impose a greater leverage upon themselves—the resistance, being on the hand, is at the farthest point. Take care in building these muscles: A kink in the shoulder point is easily sustained and difficult to get rid of.

The deltoids, like the latissimus dorsi and trapezius, have short membranous and tendinous attachments and are therefore more easily developed. Muscles with long tendons, such as those of the forearms, the backs of the thighs, and the calves, are more difficult to develop owing to their short, muscular "belly" and long, sinewy pull. Nevertheless, it is the long tendons that take the strain off the muscles and give them the endurance that the forearm and calves have in such abundance.

Broad, powerfully developed shoulders are the hallmark of the successful bodybuilder and athlete. There is nothing that sets the shoulders and chest off to better advantage than these cup-shaped mounds of muscle.

Arm Muscles

There are four muscles in the upper arms, twenty-two in the forearms, and eighteen in the hand. Study the body charts that follow on page 8 and note the names and positions of the arm muscles. It is important to remember, when practicing exercises for your upper arms,

1. Trapezius
2. Sternocleidomastoid
3. Deltoids
4. Triceps
5. Biceps
6. Forearm
7. Wrist
8. Rhomboideus
9. Latissimus Dorsi
10. Spinal Erector
11. Glueteus Maximus
12. Rectus Femoris
13. Gastrocnemius
14. Soleus
15. Achilles Tendon
16. Pectoralis Major
17. Serratus Magnus
18. External Oblique
19. Rectus Abdominis
20. Vastus Externus
21. Sartorius
22. Rectus Femoris
23. Vastus Internus
24. Tibialis Anticus
25. Peroneous Longus

that the balance of triceps and biceps is essential. No matter how large your biceps becomes, if it lacks the correlative triceps development, the physical ability of your arms will be inferior to that of the person who has a much smaller arm with a better balanced appearance.

The forearm is composed of numerous long, ribbonlike muscles, and all of them work together in gripping and hand-squeezing actions. It takes a variety of exercises to bring about the proper development and growth.

Latissimus Dorsi Muscles

As the spinal erector muscles ascend the spine they taper off, depending on the other back muscles for cooperation. Of these other back muscles, the lattissimus dorsi are the largest and most powerful.

The lattissimus dorsi cover the major portion of the back, extending upward from the lower sacral vertebrae and tapering off into the strong tendon attached to the underside of the humerus, or upper-arm bone, permitting the twist of the shoulders and back as they correlate with the functions of the arm and chest muscles. In their highly developed state, the lattissimus dorsi add to the impressiveness of the physique, as they accentuate the broadness of the shoulders, the narrowness of the waist, and the greater width of the front of the upper body.

Spinal Erector Muscles

The muscles of the small of the back called the spinal erector muscles, require careful training because they lack the bony support provided for other muscles. Toxic secretions also seem to invade and remain within the lumbar sector of the spinal erector muscles, as evidenced by the prevalence of lower-back ache. Nevertheless, the spinal erector muscles are powerful and readily respond to exercise.

These muscles are among the most important to develop because of their influence on the spine and their connection with the pelvis. It is the pelvis that bears the greatest pressure of the body weight and takes the strain of the constant bending and turning of the body.

Naturally, from the constant, diversified movements, a greater amount of waste products accumulate within these muscles than elsewhere. Obese persons tire the most quickly, because they are forced to carry the body behind the central line of natural equilibrium in order to balance the body against the drag of excessive abdominal weight. Consequently, exercise that strengthens the spinal erector muscles and frees the tissues of toxic conditions is extremely beneficial.

Only by employing every variety of progressive graduated resistance can the fullest power and development of these muscles be assured.

They run down each side of the spine like two great pillars from the base of the skull to the lowest extremity of the vertebral column, with the spine lying between them in a pronounced channel.

Gluteal Muscles

The gluteal muscles, forming the seat of the buttocks, contain more fatty substance within the muscular tissues than any others. Women tend to have a greater fatty accumulation than men. Anatomically speaking, this flesh was meant to be muscle, not padding.

The appearance and health of the body are influenced by the gluteal muscles. They are so correlated in function with the upper and lower body that they help to stabilize posture and influence leg movements such as walking, running, and climbing. The physical condition of the gluteal region determines the contour of the thighs at the hips as well as of the buttocks themselves.

Hamstring Muscles

The three hamstring muscles, or the biceps of the thighs formed on the posterior side, are short-bellied with long sinews. Rarely do they develop to the same degree as other muscles. Only those who employ the legs extremely vigorously—for example, sprinters, high jumpers, and high-kick dancers—display unusual contours of these muscles. They influence the leg in its backward movement, just as the quadriceps influence the leg in the forward movement.

Powerful thigh development adds enormously to the appearance of the physique. The progressive, graduated weight-training exercises that go to produce their size and power induce deep respiration, thereby improving the working efficiency of the internal organs and aiding total-body progress.

Calf Muscles

Calf muscles are mainly represented by the gastrocnemius muscles, which form the bulk of the calf on the posterior side. They are twin-headed muscles, dividing into two parts, the inside section usually showing less development on the average person than the outside part. This is because on the outside of the calf there are several other muscles that aid the outer section of the gastrocnemius, chief among these being the soleus. This acts with the gastrocnemius and the Achilles tendon in extension of the lower leg and foot. The tibialis anticus, or shinbone muscle, governs flexion of the foot. Never pronouncedly developed, it is an important factor in the leg. Like the peroneal muscle on the side of the calf, it is a long, ribbonlike muscle with a short belly and long tendon, though more heavily constructed than the peroneal. The sartorius of the thigh is also a long, ribbonlike muscle, but is almost all muscle from origin to insertion—that is, it has a short tendon attachment. It is often referred to as the scissors, or tailor's, muscle, because it provides a binding support to other frontal thigh muscles. This muscle is used in crossing one leg over the other and is greatly developed among wrestlers who practice the scissors hold, and also among dancers.

Proper calf development is important to the bodybuilder, for it provides both bulk and shape to the lower leg.

Pectoralis Muscles and Serratus Magnus

The pectoralis, or breast armor plates, are in two sections: minor and major. They function when squeezed together, resisting crushing pressure. People with sunken or hollow chests are showing a great deficiency in the development of the pectoralis muscles. When developed, these build the chest high, permitting fuller and better breathing. The serratus magnus of the chest sustains the depth of the lower chest and provides a greater width of the diaphragm. These muscles resemble sawteeth, and are often referred to as the sawtooth muscles. They lie alongside the ribs and have a natural tendency to pull outward on the ribs. Poor development of these muscles is indicated by a narrow chest. The lower ribs fall in, providing less space for the stomach, which causes stomach prolapse. This condition is easily remedied by widening the lower rib spaces through exercise and breathing from the diaphragm.

Bodybuilding fashions change. A few years ago it was the man with the comparatively slim but well-muscled build who was taking the physique honors. Today, the reverse is the case; bulk is considered one of the most desirable assets, with thick slabs of muscle on the chest. Fortunately, the pectorals respond fairly easily to progressive training and a few weeks of intensive effort on the various forms of bench-pressing and dipping movements will produce most desirable results. Do not undertake intensive pec building if your posture is faulty.

Abdominal Muscles

We now come to the abdominal muscles, which mean so much to your internal health. They originate under the diaphragm of the chest, known as the thoracic arch, and are embedded in a membranous sheet with a membranous attachment under the chest, at each side, and at the floor of the pubic bone. These muscles emaciate or degenerate more readily than any other group of muscles in the body. The first three rows of muscles are squarish, terminating about the line of the navel; the lower pair are long and taper off narrowly at the seat of attachment. This last pair is most subject to degeneration from lack of exercise, accumulation of surplus flesh, and from that internal bulking of the intestinal contents which makes for an obese abdomen and prolapse of the abdomen.

The moment the abdomen begins to sag and accumulate surplus flesh is the time when the level of general health begins to lower. Fat makes its first inroads upon the body on the midsection, mainly below the line of the navel, softening the muscles with its corrosion. Too much sitting is mainly responsible for this condition, depriving the abdomen of the muscular activity so important to the intestinal system. Sitting causes the abdomen between the chest and the pubic bone to contract, which allows the intestinal contents to bulk against the muscular structure, and stretch the gradually weakening tissue until little resistance remains. Nevertheless, the abdominal muscles are readily responsive to exercise. Exercise does not always develop the muscular corrugation so popular with young bodybuilders, but this high degree of development is not necessary to reinstate the former muscular vigor and tone. Some people have much heavier skin than others, in which case no amount of development will display the superdeveloped definition.

Total abdominal work for the entire midsection may seem dull and difficult at times, and the results cannot be measured in inches, but it is vitally necessary and the bodybuilder or athlete with a fine midsection displays the stamp of the well-trained person.

Oblique Muscles

The three oblique muscles lie upon each other, forming the flanks. The external oblique and the internal oblique run down through the groin into the space between the lower abdominals and the hipbone. The transversalis, or transverse oblique, is attached to the ribs and runs forward. These muscles are extremely important to both the abdominal muscles and those of the lower back, but they are often sadly neglected. Men and women who develop the oblique and lower abdominal muscles properly will be less likely to suffer ruptures in the groin.

Quadriceps Femoris Muscles

The major muscles forming the front of the thighs are the quadriceps femoris, fourfold muscles that unite into one broad tendon just above the knee and taper off to become attached below the knee on the shinbone. They are reputed to be the most powerful muscles in the body. Because of their size and great natural strength, many people think that these muscles can stand severe exercise treatment. The important point to remember about these muscles is that, next to the calf muscles, they are farthest from the heart. Under the stress of physical activity, the heart has to pump more vigorously to supply the necessary blood fuel to them.

You can easily test this by feeling the increased beat of your heart when you run or climb steps. For this reason, we should use careful judgment when treating these muscles. If you have a weak heart, avoid exercise involving vigorous activity of the thighs. The muscles of the thighs are less responsive to development than the upper-body muscles, because their fibers are almost as dense as those of the calves.

A muscle should be used in all ways that nature designed. Resistance should be provided against its natural direction of pull, and whenever possible, the complete range of motion should be employed.

For bodybuilding purposes, muscles should be exercised in a progressive, graduated manner. Work results in increased size. No work, no increase. If you strain at a weight you cannot lift, no work is done; no increase in size will follow, because the tension set up is merely dissipated as heat. Your motto should always be, "to train and never to strain." The difference between training and straining can be evaluated by the trained, mature athlete.

3

Your Conditioning Program

A good way to prepare yourself for weight training is with a well-organized series of conditioning exercises. If you haven't done much physical activity lately, you can't expect your body suddenly to be able to perform great feats of strength and agility. Just as a concert pianist must begin with a few simple finger exercises, so any serious exercise program always begins with a preliminary routine. They are exercises that you will use throughout your weight training career.

During the first week of your program, you are going to prepare your body for the more specialized work and more strenuous weight-training routines to follow in subsequent weeks. Whatever you do, don't strain yourself. If you find you are getting tired before you can complete all the routines, stop and relax. Reduce the counts for the routines you still have left, and on the next day, try to increase the counts until you've gradually done the minimum. If, on the other hand, the counts don't give you as much exercise as you want, add a few more each day. This routine is yours—so make it work for you.

Within a few days, one big factor will be obvious: You will discover how much you needed physical exercise. All at once you're getting muscles to work that have remained unused for a long, long time. Some muscle areas may ache a little. This is the sign that your routine is giving you a good fitness workout.

You can use this conditioning routine for three to four weeks before beginning weight training. This will help you build muscle size and power. In fact, those of you who desire to exercise for health purposes only, to stimulate the circulation, build the power of the heart and lungs, and keep the inner and outer musculature in first-class condition, can profitably use the conditioning program alone by exercising every day (or at least six days a week), gradually increasing the intensity of effort. You can make this type of routine more effective and interesting by gradually adding exercises from Chapters 8, 10, and 14. This will give you an excellent conditioning program. (A holiday once a week is advisable to prevent physical and mental staleness.)

Of course, if you are a serious weight-training student, you will want to use these exercises as a basis from which to build.

This conditioning program has been recommended by the President's Council on Physical Fitness and Sports. After a checkup and your physician's OK, you can proceed with these mild exercises confidently. Start gradually to avoid discomfort in muscles that have not been used consistently. Proceed at your own pace. If you find yourself at first unable to do all the repetitions called for, stop, rest, then continue. You are competing with no one but yourself.

- *Perform each exercise correctly.* As you master the various exercises, gradually step up the rate at which you perform them. This will provide greater stimulation for the circulatory and respiratory systems. Breathing and heart rate should have returned to normal ten minutes after you stop exercising.

    Women who are beginning an exercise program for the first time (or who have not engaged in serious exercise for a while) may wish to set themselves slightly lower warm-up goals in the beginning. However, as you progress in your program, you will be surprised at how much you are really capable of.
- *Exercise every day.* Pick any time that suits you best, but make these exercises a regular part of your daily routine.
- *Don't expect quick or dramatic results.* It takes time to limber up and go through the exercises without tiring. But as you continue your workouts, you will begin to feel the tonic effect of exercise— a new ease with which you do your daily work, with more energy left at the end of the day.
- *Don't get discouraged.* At first, the exercises may seem strenuous and demanding. They will seem easier with succeeding workouts.

Three general types of exercise are included: warm-up exercises, conditioning exercises, and circulatory activities.

- *Warm-up exercises* stretch the muscles, speed up the action of the heart and lungs, prepare the body for greater exertion, and reduce the possibility of strain. (See pages 17 to 20.)
- *Conditioning exercises* tone up abdominal, back, leg, and other major muscles. (See pages 21 to 23.)
- *Circulatory activities* (walking, jumping rope, running in place) contract large muscle groups for relatively longer periods than the conditioning exercises. They stimulate and strengthen the circulatory and respiratory systems. (See page 25.)

After you have become proficient in doing the warm-up exercises in the series, move on to the more strenuous exercises. Your immediate objective is to reach the point where you can do all the exercises called for, at least ten to fifteen times, without resting between exercises. Start with fewer repetitions and work up to the goal, but don't

Warm-Up Exercises

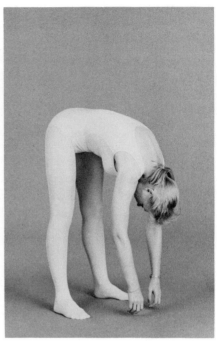

Bends and Stretches. Above, left to right: Stand erect, feet shoulder-width apart. Count 1. Bend trunk forward and down, flexing knees. Stretch gently in attempt to touch fingers to toes or floor. Count 2. Return to starting position.

NOTE: Do slowly, stretch and relax at intervals, not in rhythm.

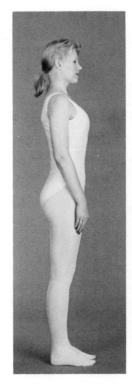

Knee Lifts. To the right: Stand erect, feet together, arms at sides. Count 1. Raise left knee as high as possible, grasping leg with hands and pulling knee against body while keeping back straight. Count 2. Lower to starting position. Counts 3 and 4. Repeat with right knee.

Wing Stretchers. Stand erect, elbows at shoulder height, fists clenched in front of chest. Count 1. Thrust elbows backward vigorously without arching back. Keep head erect, elbows at shoulder height. Count 2. Return to starting position.

Half Knee Bends. Stand erect, hands on hips. Count 1. Bend knees halfway while extending arms forward, palms down. Count 2. Return to starting position.

Arm Circles. Stand erect, arms extended sideward at shoulder height, palms up. Describe small circles, backward with hands. Keep head erect. Do fifteen backward circles. Reverse, turn palms down, and do fifteen small circles forward.

Body Benders. Stand, feet shoulder-width apart, hands behind neck, fingers interlaced. Count 1. Bend trunk sideward to left as far as possible, keeping hands behind neck. Count 2. Return to starting position. Counts 3 and 4. Repeat to the right.

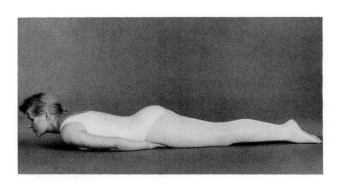 

Prone Arch. Lie face down, hands tucked under thighs. Count 1. Raise head, shoulders, and legs from floor. Count 2. Return to starting position.

omit any exercise. As soon as you are able to do this for three consecutive workouts, you are ready to move on to the conditioning program.

NOTE: People with lower-back problems should ask their doctor whether it is OK to do the Prone Arch, shown above.

Once you move past the first eleven exercises, it would be wise to preface the progressive conditioning program with the first six warm-up exercises.

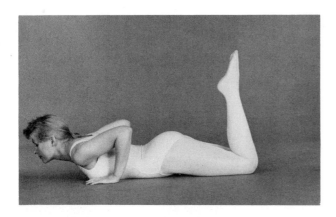 

Knee Push-Ups. Lie on floor, face down, legs together, knees bent, with feet raised off floor, hands on floor under shoulders, **palms down.** Count 1. Push upper body off floor until arms are fully extended and body is in straight line from head to knees. Count 2. Return to starting position.

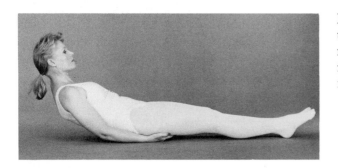

Head and Shoulder Curls. Lie on back, hands tucked under small of back. Count 1. Tighten abdominal muscles, lift head and pull shoulders and elbows off floor. Hold for four seconds. Count 2. Return to starting position.

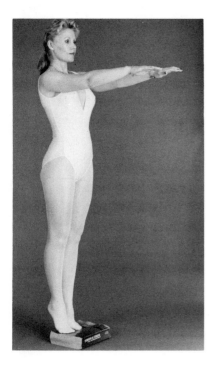

Ankle Stretches. Stand on a stair, large book, or block of wood, with weight on balls of feet and heels raised. Count 1. Lower heels. Count 2. Raise heels.

Circulatory Activities. Choose one each workout: Walking (start lively, swing arms, breathe deeply)—half mile. Skipping rope (or skipping or jumping of any type), gradually increase tempo as skill increases—skip fifteen seconds, rest sixty seconds, do three sets.

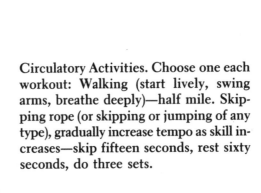

Conditioning Exercises

Toe Touches. To the left and above: Stand at attention. Count 1. Bend trunk forward and down keeping knees straight, touching fingers to ankles. Count 2. Touch fingers to top of feet. Count 3. Touch fingers to toes. Count 4. Return to starting position.

Sitting Stretches. Sit, legs spread apart, hands on knees. Count 1. Bend forward at waist, extending arms as far as possible. Count 2. Return to starting position.

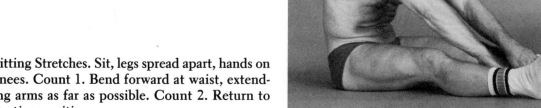

Push-Ups. To the left and below: Lie on floor, face down, legs together, hands on floor under shoulder with fingers pointing straight ahead. Count 1. Push body off floor by extending arms, so that weight rests on hands and toes. Count 2. Lower the body until chest touches floor. NOTE: Body should be kept straight, buttocks should not be raised, abdomen should not sag.

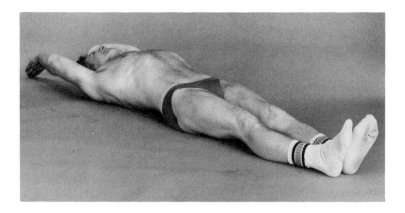

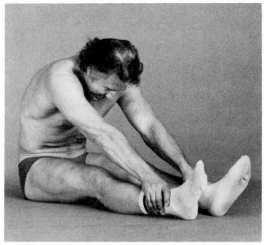

Sit-Ups (Arms Extended). Above and to the right: Lie on back, legs straight and together, arms extended beyond head. Count 1. Bring arms forward over head, roll up to sitting position, sliding hands along legs, grasping ankles. Count 2. Roll back to starting position.

Leg Raises. Right side of body on floor, head resting on right arm. Lift left leg about two feet off floor, then lower it.

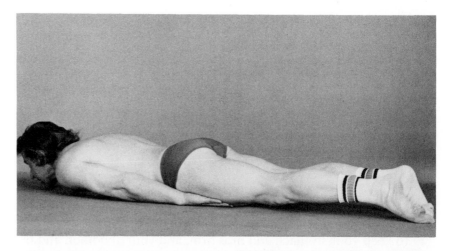

Flutter Kicks. Lie face down, hands tucked under thighs. Arch the back, bringing chest and head up, then flutter-kick continuously, moving legs eight to ten inches up and down. Kick from hips with knees slightly bent. Count each kick as one.

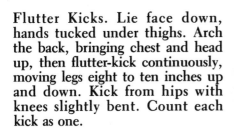

Posture

One of the basic requirements for enhancing your health, strength, and appearance is good posture. Good posture helps avoid cramping of internal organs, permits better circulation, and prevents undue tensing of some muscles and undue lengthening of others.

As you go about your daily routine, practice perfect posture. Think about your posture and align your body correctly. You may be surprised to find your attitude toward life, and people's attitudes toward you, changing for the better. Good posture brings psychological as well as physical improvement. Always endeavor to "walk tall"—the person who carries him- or herself well always looks slimmer, younger, and more smartly dressed.

Once you get the feel of proper posture, practice it until it becomes second nature.

Sitting

Sit tall and back, with your hips touching the back of the chair and your feet flat on the floor. Your chest should be out and the back of your neck nearly in line with your upper back. (When writing, lean forward from the hips so your head and shoulders are in line.)

Standing

Stand with your feet parallel, about shoulder-width apart. Your head should be high, as if you were balancing a book, and your chest out. Try to keep your stomach and hips firm, and your abdomen and back as flat as possible. Your knees should be very lightly flexed, not stiffly locked, and your weight distributed evenly on both feet, with most of it on the balls of the feet.

Walking

Begin with your knees and ankles limber, the toes pointed straight ahead, and your head and chest high. Swing your legs directly forward from the hip joints. Push your feet off the ground—don't shuffle. Swing your shoulders and arms freely and easily.

Circulatory Activities.

Walking: 120 steps per minute for one mile, swing arms and breathe deeply.
Skipping rope: Skip thirty seconds, rest thirty seconds, do three sets.
Running in place: Run sixty steps, straddle-hop ten steps.

To run in place, raise each foot at least four inches off floor and jog in place. Count one each time left foot touches floor. Complete the number of running steps called for, then do specified number of hops. To do straddle hops (also called jumping jacks), stand erect. On first count, swing arms sideward and upward, touching hands above head (arms straight) while simultaneously moving feet sideways and apart in a single jumping motion. On count of two, spring back to starting position. Each hop as two counts.

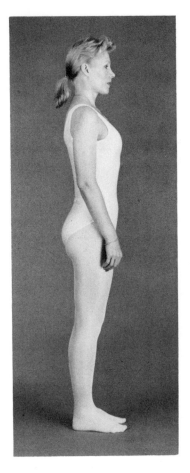

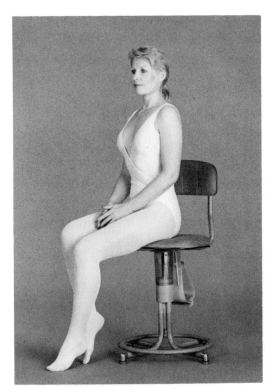

Standing.
1. Feet parallel, about six inches apart.
2. Head high, as if balancing a book.
3. Chest out.
4. Stomach and hips firm.
5. Abdomen and back as flat as possible.
6. Knees very lightly flexed—not stiffly locked.
7. Weight evenly distributed on both feet—most of it on balls of feet.

Sitting.
1. Sit tall and back, with hips touching the back of the chair, feet flat on floor.
2. Chest out, back of neck nearly in line with upper back.
3. When writing, lean forward from the hips so you keep head and shoulder in line.

4

Weight Training —What You Should Know

A great deal of evidence supports the contention that progressive barbell and dumbbell exercise is the best way to strengthen and develop the muscular structure of the human body. This applies whether your objective is to train for greater strength, for super shapeliness or for better health and general physical efficiency.

The joy of weight training and weight lifting for all enthusiasts lies not in the weight training itself but in the muscles and the total physique it develops. With intelligently applied instruction you can constantly improve at any age.

In the Beginning

Beginners should always start with a weight that is well within their physical ability to handle. During your first several weeks, your muscular tissues will go through a form of transition, and your organs will go through a toning process. The muscles and organs are more or less below par at this point. The fibers of the muscles are loosely or coarsely constructed and are incapable of complete contraction. The tendons lack pulling power from the muscles. The circulation is below par and the lungs are below their natural respiratory level. The stomach muscles and those of the abdomen are probably not what they should be, and neither are the muscles that support the walls of the chest. Therefore, in order to tone and improve and overcome these conditions so that more vigorous exercise can be beneficially applied, all these deficiencies should gradually be eliminated.

Care is required during the early stages of training. If something should happen that retards progress, and if the muscles are forced before the conditioning process has taken place, development may be greatly delayed. The internal organs may be flaccid and not respond as quickly as do the external muscles, so give great care to this consideration. In order to be sure that nothing will happen that may retard progress, the weight of the barbell or dumbbells should be within your capacity to handle without straining yourself. Breathing exercises should predominate, with exercises that involve bending and straightening the body, and stretching the muscles to the limit of their natural capacity. Gradually you can get the body into shape and accustom it to the natural progressive exercise routines that follow.

Exercise of this nature should be practiced daily during the first month. Results may not become apparent to the eye; nevertheless, the organs and concealed muscles improve in condition as will the external musculature.

The compact nature of the muscles is what causes greater muscular contraction and extension; as this takes place, increased development begins and continues. The organs respond better to gentler treatment than do the muscles. The proper consideration given to the chest and abdomen during the early stages will give wonderful benefits for the internal organs, making them more responsive to muscular demand during growth.

Remember, the law of health and physical development depends upon the conservation of energy, the replenishment of broken-down tissue, and the nutrition of the cells. The foundation for these vital factors depends upon how you treat the organs and the muscles during your preliminary training stages. Heavy weights used at the beginning will retard the stimulation of these three important factors. Always subject the amount of weight used to the capabilities of the body. Never subordinate the body to the weight.

This toning program is recommended for at least one month, but those who know they are physically below par should devote more time, possibly three months, to this important conditioning process.

A Few Pointers

After this procedure, increase the amount of weight per exercise and start out on a real bodybuilding program. More than twelve exercises should not be employed during one exercise period, and you should work out every other day, Monday, Wednesday, Friday, or Sunday, Tuesday, and so on. The exercises should cover every part of the body. Give the body a chance to warm up. The exercises involving heavier weights should begin with the third or fourth exercise. Never start with a heavy exercise. Finish up your exercise period with an abdominal exercise. This brings the greatest flow of blood back to where it is most needed.

Breathing Is Important

Breathing is very important during exercise. You should always breathe in and out rhythmically. Your lungs are the main conveyors of oxygen into your body. The more oxygen brought into your body during exercise, the greater is the body fertilized. Breathe in wherever you expend the greatest effort during the exercise and breathe out as you relax. Do not be in any hurry to increase your poundage per exercise or your repetitions per exercise. Not until your body has become fully prepared for this measure should a definite routine of increase in weight and repetition take place.

Progressive Weight Training

All courses call for a set progressive scale of weight and repetition increase until a certain limit is reached. Then you are advised to increase your poundage per exercise and start over with the original count and work up as before. Nevertheless, all exercise cannot be subjected to a set rule of increase in repetition and in weight. Some exercises should stop at a certain count. After that count is reached there is no value in practicing more repetitions. The exercise will change from a muscular movement to a nervous or stress movement, and you must always avoid strain.

Numerous exercises can be progressively used. After the limit is reached in one group, you can graduate to the more progressive group. Therein is the value of exercise, but each exercise must be worked on until all its value is reduced.

The value of intelligently applied progressive weight-resistance exercise is that it does the most good in the shortest time without wasting energy and with no stress or nervous reaction. Only when you are using too much weight or too many repetitions, or advancing too fast into the advanced grades, will a nervous reaction take place. Improvement cannot come from such a procedure, and this is responsible for most failures, along with the fact that many people practice the exercise incorrectly.

Enthusiasm, while a great asset, is a detriment to success in many cases. We need enthusiasm, but tempered with good judgment and with strict adherence to a proper routine.

Specialization

Specialization should not be practiced until you have gone through the entire training program. Then your defects will be more clearly seen, as will those parts of your body that respond easily. Each person differs. When you are ready for specialization, you can practice a number of exercises covering a particular part of your body. Practice advanced exercise only after all other training stages have been exhausted and your body is well balanced and built for the advanced system of training. This is the only time you should really use substantial weights for an exercise, but you should cut down on repetitions. If you have faith-fully followed the advice given herein, you can safely work out to your limit.

Pitfalls of Weight Lifting and Bodybuilding

Practicing the sport of weight lifting is something different. Weight lifting is not simply a bodybuilding exercise but a sport in which tech-nique plays a big part. Before commencing the sport of lifting weights, see that your body is fully capable of doing so.

Remember that a barbell or a pair of dumbbells in your hands is only a piece of apparatus. The important part is the arrangement of exercises and how each shall be progressed upon. Only this will safely graduate the development of the body and build those mighty organic reservoirs of power and energy from which the muscles draw their nutri-tion and vigor. Too many bodybuilders are engrossed with the building of muscles only. The wise bodybuilder lays his or her foundation from the inside.

It is a fact that you can build the muscles of the body while disre-garding the internal organs, with the result that you can perform a feat that is not beyond the capacity of your muscular power but *is* beyond the ability of your internal organs. This causes strain or an organic weakening that will show up sooner or later in life.

Rest

Increase of muscular size is the result of a certain balance between exercise, nourishment, and rest. Progressive exercise stimulates growth, food provides the material for that growth, and during periods of rest and sleep the actual growth takes place. The secret of success in body-building is to be certain that all these factors are present in the proper degree. Therefore, be sure to get sufficient sleep, rest, and relaxation. Get out of the customary modern habit of late hours, and try to get to bed early each night. If you try to combine strenuous muscle-building with late-night activities, you will fail to get the best results, and you will have only yourself to blame. A good restful night's sleep rejuvenates your system, wipes away tired lines from your face, and eliminates body fatigue.

It is especially important to rest whenever you find yourself going stale. It is easy to tell when this happens: you feel burned out, low in energy, look with distaste upon your work, and generally feel dull and dispirited. Every athlete goes stale occasionally. Rest until your energy is completely restored before resuming your exercises, and learn to anticipate the need of a letup before it becomes absolutely necessary.

Sometimes a condition of toxicity, due to faulty nutrition, constipation, poor ventilation, or insufficient sleep, may produce a lethargy very similar to staleness. Through practice, you will soon learn how to recognize these conditions and how best to combat them.

Your Aim Should Be . . .

A strong body with fine muscle tone is the aim of every athlete. Muscle tone means having flexible muscles in top condition that quickly respond in speed, strength, and coordination to the needs of every sport. Where once the sole aim was to create big muscles through weight lifting, barbells have now been found to be the ideal bodybuilder for all modern sports, for they are the quickest, surest way to train.

Follow the instructions in this book carefully and you will receive the full benefits from this wonderful means of building a strong, healthy body. Try to establish a routine you can faithfully follow.

5

Preliminary Weight-Training Instructions

There are many types of weight-training programs and schedules. For all practical purposes the "set" system of weight training is the most practical and effective method.

Your muscles will adjust to a certain load or resistance, so it is necessary to increase the resistance after you can complete the designated number of sets and repetitions of an exercise without strain. Your best guide is that the last repetition of each exercise should be a real effort. Never allow yourself to cheat in order to accomplish the final repetition. Perform it as correctly as you did the first repetition.

The graduated programs that follow are a practical guide, effective and easy to follow:

Program I—One set, fifteen to twenty repetitions
Program II—Two sets, ten to fifteen repetitions
Program III—Three sets, six to ten repetitions

Follow Program I for about six weeks. Then begin Program II and complete the same procedure before getting on to Program III.

Keep in mind that you do not increase the number of repetitions or sets; you increase the resistance or weight. As your skill and strength increase, add enough weight so that you must make an effort to do the exercises, *but always without strain.*

When you perform an exercise once, this is called one repetition (or one *rep*). If you do the same exercise twice in a row, this is called two repetitions (or two reps). And so on. A group of repetitions (reps) of the same exercise is called a set. If you repeat an exercise ten times in succession and then stop to rest, you have performed one set of ten repetitions.

It is important that you study the illustrations and instructions carefully. The illustrations show the exercises being perfectly performed. Don't get discouraged if you find it difficult to duplicate them. Constant practice in front of a mirror helps you to eliminate your faults by comparing your performance with the illustrations.

It is almost impossible to advise you on the correct amount of weight to use for each exercise. No two persons are alike: Age, weight, condition, and occupation differ.

You must use your own judgment, starting out with poundages per exercise well within your limits. From this point, you will learn to select the amount of weight that you can handle correctly for the scheduled number of repetitions and still complete your training session without feeling fatigued—just comfortably tired.

Keep a record of the exercises you perform, how many times you repeat them, and how much weight you are using. This will help you to maintain an accurate schedule and will give you a clear idea of the gains you make. Remember, physical fitness or physical development can be improved by gradually increasing the amount of work performed, but you must progress in easy stages. Overdoing an exercise or training program will retard progress. You should never attempt to lift a heavier weight until you have gradually trained and conditioned yourself to do so.

Do not rush through your exercises. Do them smoothly and rhythmically. When exercising a particular part of the body—such as an arm—bend it as much as possible and then straighten it as much as possible. By exercising from complete extension to flexion, you will guard against muscle shortening and gain elasticity. In addition, each of your working muscles will be exercised more completely. Consistency is probably the most important factor of all in conditioning the body. Remember to make your workout consistent for best results. And always remember: Your objective is to train, never to strain.

Adding New Exercises to Your Fitness Program

After several weeks of doing sets of repetitions as outlined, all of your major muscle groups should be in reasonably good condition. You are now ready to expand your program. Do this by adding one or two new exercises each week. Try to acquire equipment that will allow you to reach a different body part with each new exercise.

Each time you add a new exercise, start with a few reps and gradually build to a set or several sets. In this way, your working muscles will increase in strength, stamina, and endurance. The ultimate number of exercises you should perform will depend upon your physical condition, how often you train, and what your objective is.

Once you are basically in good physical condition, it doesn't matter which exercises you perform as long as they reach all of your major muscle groups and some of your lesser ones. You will come to know what each exercise does for you and will find it easy to adjust your program to your changing needs.

Special Training Hints

How Often To Exercise

Every-other-day training is suggested for your weight-training schedule (for example, Monday, Wednesday, Friday, etc.) except for the abdominal exercises and those in which you are trying to reduce size in the waist, hips, thighs, or any other trouble spots. These should be done daily. If you are thin or of normal size and weight, try to do milder forms of exercise on off-days. Walking, swimming, skating, cycling, and jogging are all beneficial.

What to Wear

Light, loose, porous training clothes are best, because they allow greater air circulation. Obtain two complete outfits so that one is always fresh and clean. For those who wish to lose weight, a sweat suit, which can be slipped over your regular gym suit, is also recommended.

When to Exercise

You may exercise at any time, provided it does not interfere with your regular meals or sleeping hours. It is best to exercise when fully rested. You should allow at least one to two hours to elapse after eating before indulging in a training session.

How Long to Exercise

The length of your workout will depend on your physical condition, how hard you train, and how much rest you take between exercises. Start with short, light, easy workouts and gradually increase. Even if you have little time to spare for exercises, that time can be valuable. Five minutes a day, properly utilized, is of far greater value than no exercise at all.

How Long to Rest

A short rest of one minute should be taken immediately after each set of repetitions you perform. Make sure that your muscles are kept warm during the short rest periods. A sweat suit is perfect for this purpose.

How to Breathe

Do not hold your breath when exercising. Try to breathe naturally. A basic rule to follow while exercising, to coordinate movement with breathing, is to inhale as the arms move away from the body or sides and to exhale as they return toward the sides or the starting position. In all waist-bending movements, exhale as you bend forward and inhale as you raise your torso to the starting position.

How to Finish Up

Take a bath or shower after you complete your exercise session. A warm shower, followed by a brisk toweling, is preferable. This will stimulate surface circulation and have a beneficial effect on your skin.

How to Choose Your Weights

To figure weight correctly, always include the weight of the bar with the collars. The standard adjustable dumbbell set, a fourteen-inch bar with collars, weighs about ten pounds. The four-foot bar without collars weighs about twelve pounds; the five-foot bar, fifteen pounds. Standard collars weigh approximately one pound; heavy-duty collars approximately two pounds. You can purchase plates or disks as light as one and one fourth pounds; these will allow you to progress slowly, without strain.

Always keep an equal amount of weights on each end and be sure the collars are tight so they cannot slip. Start with light weights. As your skill and strength increase, add enough weights so that you must make an effort to do the exercises, but always without strain.

How to Hold the Dumbbell or Barbell

There are two ways of holding a dumbbell or barbell. The undergrip (palms up) allows the bell to rest in the palm of your hand as you raise the bell. In the overgrip (palms down), you hold the bar with your knuckles above the bar and your thumbs below. The barbell is usually held with the hands shoulder-width apart.

6

Barbell Training Course

You are about to begin what has proven to be the very best method of bodybuilding. Progressive, graduated exercise intelligently applied with modern adjustable barbells and dumbbells has been recognized the world over by physical educators as being the quickest, safest, most effective method for keeping fit and developing muscular power and beauty.

With the modern adjustable barbell you can select any assortment of weight plates from one and one-quarter pounds to one hundred pounds, which makes it readily usable by anyone, however developed or undeveloped. The moderate cost of the equipment and the small space required makes it possible for everyone to experience the benefits of weight training, especially when the training program is combined with dumbbell exercises and supplementary exercises.

1. Press Position. Stand with your feet comfortably apart, back straight. Keeping your knuckles facing forward, stoop and grasp the bar. With a quick, smooth motion, swing the barbell to shoulder height, keeping your elbows well forward. Press up until your arms are fully extended. Hold for an instant; then complete the motion by lowering the barbell to shoulder position.

Training Suggestions.
• Keep your hands approximately shoulder-width apart, grasping the bar with the over-grip position, knuckles facing forward.
• Extend your arms fully.
• Keep your back in a straight flat position.
• Make sure your knees are bent to approximately 90 degrees, with your seat (buttocks) a little higher than your knee joints.
• Your head should be in a comfortable position.

This position is basic to all movements where the weight is lifted from and lowered to the floor. Proper techniques for lifting weight are important to avoid back injuries. Involves chest, trapezius, shoulder, and triceps.

As these three illustrations show, the press position is for women also.

2. Two-Hands Slow Curl. With palms forward, raise the bar from the floor to thigh level. Curl to shoulder height. Hold and complete by returning to thigh level.

Training Suggestions: Your body must remain perfectly erect throughout the movement. Try to move only your forearms, keeping your upper arms steady and close to your body. Involves flexor muscles of the arm, especially the biceps.

3. Rowing Motion. Keep the back flat and horizontal to the floor. Raise the bar from the floor to your chest, hold and then lower your arms back to the starting position.

Training Suggestions: Keep your legs straight or slightly bent. The barbell must be lowered to the starting position with control. Do not allow it to drop. Your body must not move out of position throughout the movement. If you find it difficult to maintain this position, rest your forehead on any support at the same height.

Involves: upper-back and arm muscles.

4. **Back Squat, or Knee Bend.** With the barbell supported on the back of your shoulders, feet comfortably apart, breathe in fully, then bend your knees and sink down to the squat position as shown. Pause very briefly, then return to the upright position, exhaling as you come up. *The back must be kept straight all the time*—this is most important!

Training Suggestions: If you find it difficult to maintain the squatting position, a block of wood or board may be placed under your heels to maintain balance throughout the movement. Deep breathing is an important part of this exercise. Inhale deeply at the start, exhale while lowering into full squat position, then inhale deeply while rising. Keep your back as straight as possible and avoid leaning forward as much as possible.

Involves: legs, buttocks, hips, back, and chest.

5. Side-to-Side Bend. To the left: Rest the bar firmly across your shoulders, behind your head. Bend sideways, alternating to right and left as far as possible. Pull your elbows into your sides.

Training Suggestions: Maintain an erect position. Do not allow your body to bend back or forward.

Involves: sides, especially the abdominals and obliques.

6. Raise on Toes. Below, left to right: Rest the bar on your shoulders. Rise up on your toes as high as possible. Hold, then lower your heels to the floor.

Training Suggestions: Your knees must not bend. This exercise can be varied in direction by turning your toes in, out, and straight ahead.

Involves: calves, ankles, feet, and arch muscles.

7. Press Behind Neck. Rest the bar on your shoulders as in exercise 5. Brace your legs and trunk, then press the bar steadily to arm's-length overhead. Hold and return the bar to your shoulders.

Training Suggestions: Maintain a good erect form without straining.

Involves: Shoulders, upper back, side trunk, and rear of upper arm.

9. **Front Raise.** Start with the bar at thigh level. Lift the bar slowly, extending your arms until it is at shoulder level. Return slowly to starting position. Keep your arms straight at all times, with your back held as straight as possible.

Training Suggestions: Keep body well braced, with arms held perfectly straight and in control throughout movement, especially in lowering weight to starting position.

Involves: deltoid, chest, and back.

8. **Hack Squat.** To the left, on the opposite page: Stand with heels on a one-inch block or a weight plate. Squat and grasp the bar. Raise by straightening your legs to a full standing position. Slowly squat, and repeat.

Training Suggestions: Use an overgrip with your palms facing backwards. The bar should be held full-length just below your buttocks. Without arching your back, bend your knees and lower your body as far as you can, keeping your heels flat and arms straight. Keep your balance.

Involves: Thighs, hips, and buttocks.

10. Seated Press. Above and to the right: Bring the bar to chest height with your palms forward. Rest the bar on your chest, then press overhead and slightly back. Hold, and return to chest-high position.

Training Suggestions: Keep an erect position. Do not slouch. Push steadily, evenly.

Involves: arms, shoulders, and back.

12. **Straight-Arm Pullover.** Lie on the floor or bench with your arms straight back. Grasp the bar and pull overhead in one motion, forward and down to rest on your upper legs. Then return slowly to the starting point.

Training Suggestions: Keep your arms rigid throughout the movement. Inhale fully while grasping the bar, then exhale slowly and completely while lowering the barbell to your knees. Then inhale slowly and completely back to the starting position.

Involves: chest and shoulders; greatly assists in the stretching and mobility of the chest.

11. **Upright Rowing.** To the left: Stand erect, chest held high, your feet approximately hip-width apart, with the weight held at the "hang" position in front of your thighs. Overgrip with your hands about six to eight inches apart. Pull the weight strongly upward by bending both of your elbows and raising them sideways and upward until the bar is close to your chin, at the top of your chest.

Training Suggestions: Inhale slowly as you lift upward, and exhale as you lower the weight to the starting position. Do not swing the weight upward. Maintain a firm grip as you lower it back to the starting position.

Involves: shoulders, upper back, rear of arm, and flexors of elbow joint.

13. Bent-Arm Pullover. Lie on a bench and hook your legs securely around the bench legs. Reach back with your arms and lift the bar upward and over your chest. Lower the bar back slowly until below head. Hold. Return to the beginning.

Training Suggestions: Overgrip palms up, with your hands approximately shoulder-width apart. Inhale as the weight is lowered behind your head. Exhale when returning to the overhead position. Try to keep your elbow joints at right angles throughout the movement. You must always be in complete control of the down movement without straining.

Involves: Chest, shoulder girdle, and large muscles of the lower back.

14. Press on Bench. Lie on a bench with the bar resting on your chest. Grasp the bar and press upward until your arms are fully extended. Hold, then lower to starting position.

Training Suggestions: Make sure that you are firmly balanced on the bench. Hold the bar with your hands approximately shoulder-width apart, palms up. You can vary the grip by spacing your hands wider than shoulder-width apart.

Involves: all the upper-body muscles, especially the chest, front deltoids, and triceps.

CAUTION: When using maximal poundages on such exercises as squats and bench presses, training with a partner is safest.

15. Sit-Up. Lie on the floor. Place your feet beneath the bar and your hands behind your head. Sit up and forward as far as possible without bending your knees. Then return to starting position.

Training Suggestions: Exhale completely while sitting up. Inhale while returning to starting position.

Involves: stomach muscles.

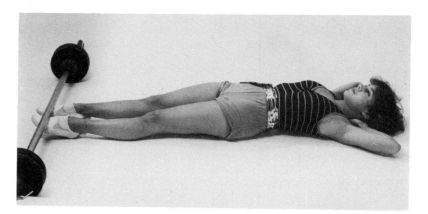

PLEASE NOTE: It is important that you gradually add exercises from Chapters 7, 8, 9, and 10 to these exercises. Progressive diversification will help to prevent boredom and speed the improvement of your body's shape and strength.

7

Dumbbell Training Course

Adjustable dumbbells and barbells are partners. Either one is incomplete without the other. A muscle or group of muscles must be strengthened from every possible angle. Every variety of exercise should be practiced.

Dumbbells are a necessary aid to barbell training; they help you to reach your limit in strength and symmetry. They are invaluable on your barbell training days to help reach muscles that cannot be developed with the barbell, or they can be used as a separate training session. The movements involved in dumbbell exercises can be selected to isolate any muscle group, so that the weaker groups can be treated as effectively as the larger and stronger groups.

The ambitious weight trainee or athlete who has plenty of endurance and ambition can use the dumbbells during a part of every barbell day, either as a partial rest between the heavier barbell exercises or to taper off after having performed all the barbell exercises. If you are this type of athlete, it is best to use the dumbbells alone on two other days. This will speed your progress and greatly increase your strength and development. On these dumbbell training days, the intent is not to limit poundages, but rather to tone your muscles and keep them prepared for the heavier barbell days to come.

If you have purchased a dumbbell set and do not yet own a barbell, it will be best for you to use heavier weights in some of the exercises as soon as you are ready.

The following dumbbell exercises are designed with the knowledge that a great many exercises must be followed to build shape, strength, and power. A few simple exercises will bring a fair degree of strength, but will not bring maximum results. Before attempting any of the exercises, reread the chapters on training so that you are aware of the correct procedures to follow. Keep perfection of performance in mind at all times.

Perform each exercise at least eight times. Try to increase by one rep each week; gradually work up to fifteen reps. Gradually add exercises from Chapters 6, 8, 9, and 10 to provide variety.

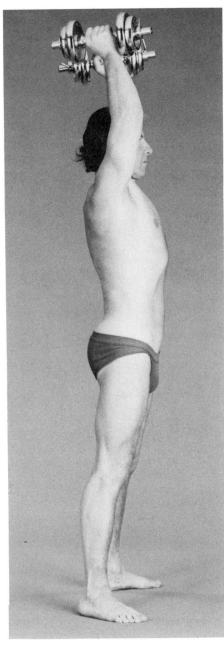

1. Two-Arm Dumbbell Swing (Warm-Up). Left to right: Stand with your feet apart and a bell in each hand. Swing them well back between your legs, then up until they are higher than your head. Repeat fully in both directions.

Training Suggestions: Keep your back as flat as possible. Keep your arms and legs straight or slightly bent. Inhale when swinging the dumbbell upwards and exhale when swinging back to the starting position.

Involves: all major body muscles.

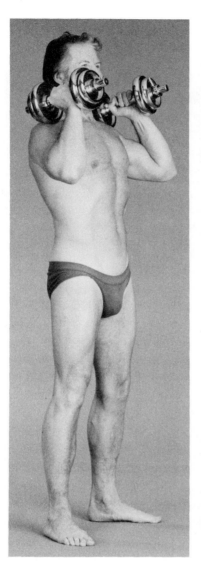  

2. Two-Arm Press. Take a bell in each hand, palms facing body. Pull them to your shoulders. Press them slowly and steadily to arm's-length overhead. Lower in same manner and repeat.

Training Suggestions: Maintain your body in a strong, well-braced position as the dumbbells are pressed to arm's-length overhead. Inhale as they are pressed overhead and exhale as they are lowered back to starting position.

Involves: shoulders, upper back, and muscles at back of upper arm.

Variation: See photograph on the far right for the alternate dumbbell press (seesaw). Begin from the same position. Start with your left hand and press the dumbbell to arm's-length. As you start to lower the dumbbell, start pressing the right hand to arm's-length overhead. Try to approximate a seesaw action. Inhale on the upward movement and exhale as you go back to starting position. As you become stronger, you will be able to handle much more weight in this press position.

Variation: From a seated position, with the dumbbells held at your shoulders, raise your arms overhead, reaching as high as possible, while inhaling deeply. As your arms descend, exhale while rounding your back. This exercise creates unusual breathing depth and tone.

3. Dumbbell Squat. Begin with your feet comfortably apart. Hold the dumbbells at shoulder height. Bend your knees and lower your body into the squat position, inhaling; as you rise back into the erect position, exhale.

Training Suggestions: Do not strain. Keep your back as flat as possible with your chest and head up. Try to breathe naturally while performing in a rhythmical manner.

Involves: legs, back, and chest. A valuable cardiovascular exercise when mastered with high repetitions.

Variation: This version requires practice and balance, and conditions the thigh muscles to juggle the body weight. Stand erect, your feet comfortably apart, the dumbbells held overhead, with palms facing front. Keeping an erect posture, slowly lower into a sitting position on your toes. Without pausing, return to the starting position, maintaining balance with the dumbbells at arm's-length overhead. Breathe naturally and do not strain.

Variation: This is one of the best leg exercises, quite a bit harder than the squat exercise. Perform the knee bend on your toes, with your heels together and knees wide apart. You cannot use as much weight as in the squat style.

4. Toe Raise. Stand erect. Hold a dumbbell at thigh level in each hand, palms facing thighs. Rise high on your toes. Lower your heels to the floor and repeat.

Training Suggestions: Keep your body perfectly erect throughout the movement. Inhale as you raise your body and exhale as you lower your heels to the floor.

Involves: lower leg muscles, especially calves.

Variation: Place your toes and the balls of your feet on a block of wood about two inches high, resting your heel on the floor. Perform in the same manner.

5. Two-Arm Curl. Stand erect, holding your arms straight at your sides. Hold the dumbbells with the palms of your hands facing forward. Very slowly, bend your forearms upward to your shoulders. Inhale slowly on the upward movement and exhale on extending your arms back to the starting position.

Training Suggestions: Keep your upper arms stationary. Do not grip the sides of your body with your upper arms or allow your elbows to rest on your body. The more you turn your thumbs away from your body as you are curling the bells, the greater the resistance on your biceps muscles.

Involves: upper-front arm muscles—the biceps and the elbow flexor muscles.

Variation: The alternate-arm curl, performed in exactly the same style. Curl one dumbbell to your shoulder. As you begin to lower the bell back to starting position, start to curl the other bell to your shoulder.

Variation: Curl the weight to your shoulder with palms up, keeping the upper arm close to the body. In lowering, your forearm should rotate to a palms-down position, and your hands should be forced well out to the sides. Remember to keep your elbows close to your body. This movement is excellent for the muscles that flex the elbow joint and greatly affects the wrist and forearms.

Variation: Two-arm reverse curl. This movement is performed with exactly the same style—only this time you use the overgrip on holding the dumbbells.

6. Triceps Press (Single-Arm Version). Left to right: This may be carried out standing or in the seated position. With your trunk erect, press a dumbbell to arm's-length overhead. For steadiness, your free hand may be folded across your chest, gripping the opposite side. Keeping your upper arm vertical and steady, completely bend the arm, lowering the weight down to a position behind the head. Vigorously restraighten the arm.

Training Suggestions: Keep your posture well braced and your elbow pointing upward during lower flexes behind the head. Breathe in and out naturally.

Involves: muscles at rear of upper arm.

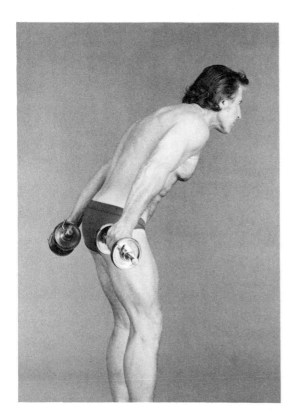

7. Triceps Extension. To the left: Stand erect, keeping your arms tight to your sides and your palms up with the thumbs turned out. Bend forward slightly. Keep your arms straight and raise them backward as far as possible. When your arms are extended to the limit, twist your hands to the right and then to the left as far as you can. Slowly return to starting position.

Training Suggestions: Be sure to keep your arms straight and tight to your side and your palms facing forward.

Involves: rear upper-arm muscles.

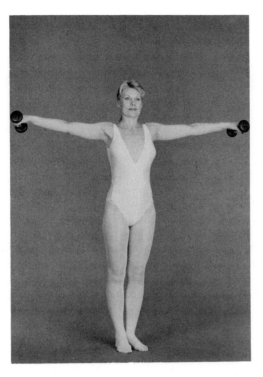 

8. Lateral Raise. Stand with your feet comfortably spaced, holding a dumbbell at each side, palms facing your body. Raise the dumbbells directly sideways to shoulder level. Hold and return to starting position.

Training Suggestions: Keep your arms straight throughout. Inhale while raising arms and exhale while lowering arms back to starting position.

Involves: upper-body musculature, mainly side shoulder (deltoid) muscles.

Variation: Hold the dumbbells with palms facing your body. This time, keeping the arms straight, raise the dumbbells to a position directly in front of your face. This influences front deltoid development.

Variation: As in the lateral raise, lean forward at the hips, back straight, and allow your arms to hang straight down from the shoulders. Keeping your arms straight, raise them directly sideways. Lower slowly to starting position and repeat.

9. Side Bend. Stand erect, a dumbbell held in each hand at thigh level. Bend directly over to your left side, exhaling. Return your upper body to an erect position while inhaling, then bend directly over to the opposite side, exhaling. Alternate bend from side to side.

Training Suggestions: Keep your body erect at all times—do not bend forward or backward.

Involves: midsection muscles, especially side waist and lower-back muscles.

10. Toe Touching. Press a dumbbell to arm's-length overhead, always keeping your eyes on the dumbbell. Spread your legs about fifteen inches apart, keeping your knees stiff throughout.

Now, with the dumbbell aloft, lower your body until your left hand can touch your foot. Raise and repeat with your other arm.

Training Suggestions: Keep proper balance; do not strain. Practice will perfect this movement.

Involves: sides of the waist and lower-back muscles.

8

Streamline Your Waistline

Perhaps no part of the human anatomy is more important to health and fitness than the waist. Here is where our muscular condition—our physical fitness—is revealed at a glance. The first and most obvious sign of physical deterioration is a bulging waistline.

Externally, the waist is a muscular wall of protection for the inner organs. Extending from the base of the breast bone to the floor of the pelvis, these abdominals, reeflike rows of muscle, along with the obliques, side waist muscles, serve mechanically in controlling the bending and twisting movements of the trunk and contributing to the correct posture of the body. It is all very well to have strong arms and a grip of steel, but what use are these unless your midsection is in perfect condition?

When your waist measurement is more than one inch larger than it should be for your frame, it is usually a sign that excess fat has accumulated. For someone in good physical condition, the male waistline should measure at least eight to ten inches less than the chest. In women the waist should measure about ten inches less than the hips. In both, sides of the waist should be evident even when completely relaxed.

To condition and rebuild the waistline, it must be muscularly stimulated. This is where the right type of exercise is of paramount importance. The instant the outer or external muscles begin to contract and relax in exercising, the internal muscles perform the same work of contracting and relaxing. Some individuals turn to diet and massage to aid in this rebuilding process. Although these measures are very helpful in eliminating fat and toxins and preventing further accumulation, they fall short of the ultimate objective.

Those folks with the unsightly bulge or "bay-window" type of waistline, known as abdominal or stomach prolapse, should practice exercises that involve lifting the legs toward the body. However, when they do, they usually and mistakenly employ those exercises where the upper part of the body is brought into close play with the lower part—for example, standing erect and trying to touch the toes with the hands without bending the knees, or lying stretched-out on the back and sitting up. These movements aggravate the condition by bulging the abdominal contents further down against the already weakened muscular structure.

The Correct Exercises

The correct exercises are those in which you lie flat on your back or, better still, on an inclined board, with your feet slightly higher than your head. This allows the stomach and abdomen to spread out naturally. When the legs lift toward the body, the abdominal contents fall inward and away from the muscular wall, thereby allowing full and unrestricted functioning of the muscles from the pelvis to the chest. Once the objective is achieved, more varied and advanced exercises can be practiced. Women who, following childbirth, find themselves with distended waistlines will especially profit from these exercises.

Those of you not afflicted with waist problems may perform exercises in all body positions. If you are thin, the exercises will tone up the digestive apparatus, enabling you to benefit more from your food and so become better nourished and developed. If you are rather corpulent, the exercises will produce excessive heat in the muscles around the waist region, burning up the fat and resulting in its gradual loss. Wearing a sweatshirt and pants will result in a faster reduction of the fat.

If you wish to obtain the fullest abdominal development, you must eventually progress to the stage that safely warrants the substitution of the most advanced exercises. As you progress in strength and development, you can use weights in the appropriate exercises. In some movements, such apparatuses as light dumbbells can be tied to the ankles, or iron boots can be employed. The latter apparatus, resembling a shoe, is the most convenient to use (see Chapter 14).

Perform the following exercises regularly and in gradually increasing amounts. A good plan is to perform at least eight reps per exercise, gradually working up to sixteen reps. You then can perform additional sets. If you cannot perform eight reps in good form, then perform within your capacity working toward said routine. The object at all times is to train and not to strain.

Allow at least two hours to elapse after eating before exercising. This gives your digestion a chance. Breathe deeply and naturally at all times. It's best to exhale with the effort and inhale as you return to the starting position. Wear as little clothing as possible to allow for freedom of motion. Watch your posture: sit straight, walk erect, and do not slouch over. The faithful performance of the exercises will help you to feel and look years younger.

You do not have to practice all of these exercises at one time. Vary them, and you will find them most interesting and beneficial. As you progress in development, you will find the muscles of the waist constitute a natural muscular corset. You will then possess a trim, hard, muscular waistline.

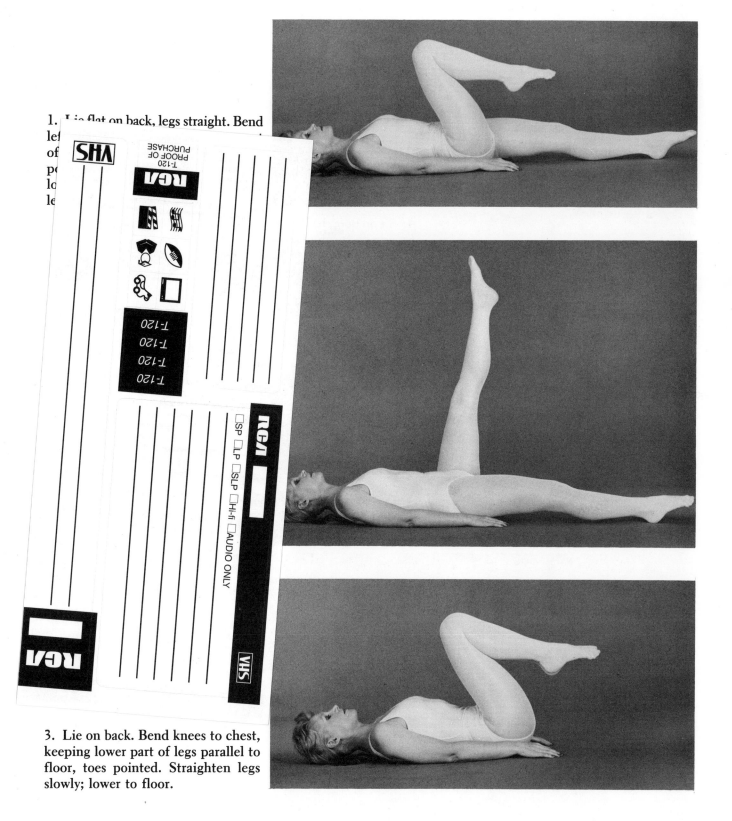

1. Lie flat on back, legs straight. Bend
lef...
of...
p...
lo...
le...

3. Lie on back. Bend knees to chest,
keeping lower part of legs parallel to
floor, toes pointed. Straighten legs
slowly; lower to floor.

4. Sit on floor, hands clasped behind neck. Twist trunk from side to side by turning left and right as far as body will go.

5. Lie on back, legs straight. Raise heels three inches off floor. Scissor legs as in swimming. Continue to flutter-kick until you feel a strain. Lower legs to floor. Relax.

Variation: Instead of scissoring legs, spread them apart and bring together until strain is felt. Lower to floor.

6. Sit on floor, arms stretched forward. Reach for toes gradually, then let hands slide up legs to thighs as you lower upper body to floor. Keep back rounded as you go down. Come up slowly and again reach for toes. Repeat.

Variation: Place hands behind neck. Pull head down to legs, trying to touch face to knees. Lower. Raise again to sitting position.

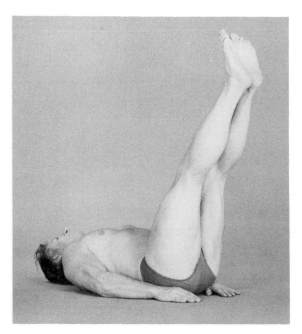

7. Lie flat on your back, arms on floor at sides, palms down. Keep legs straight, raise them slowly until perpendicular, then lower slowly to original position. Repeat until you feel a strain. Rest. Repeat.

Variation: Instead of stopping feet while perpendicular, bring them back until they touch floor behind head. To do this, press down on floor with hands, raise lower back from floor.

8. Lie on back, hands on thighs. Sit up; at same time, raise legs off floor. Stretch hands forward towards toes. Try to hold this position and then lower body and legs slowly back to starting position.

9. Lie on back, feet held down by a partner or hooked under edge of dresser. Place hands behind neck. Sit up slowly, curling forward as you do so. Lower to lying position by slowly uncurling upper body.

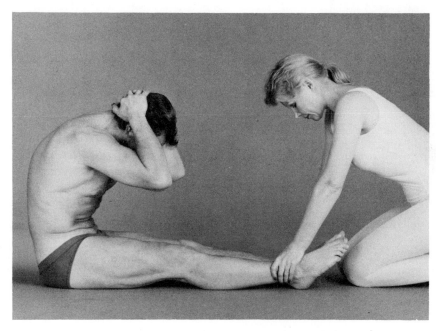

A

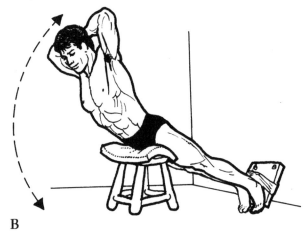

B

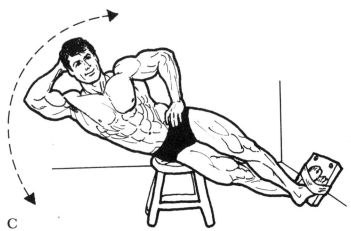

C

10. Advanced. (A) Sit on stool or side of chair placed about two feet from edge of bed (or the special apparatus shown in the figure). Hook your feet under edge of bed or use special apparatus. Bend backward as far as possible, keeping your hands clasped on your waist. Return to a sitting position. More effective: Place your hands behind your neck. Relax between attempts. Continue until tired. This exercise can be performed in other positions as shown for developing other muscles about the waist, such as sitting sideways (C) or face down (B).

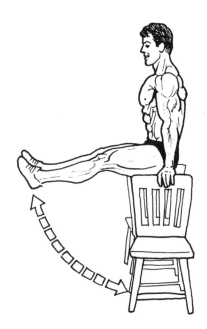

11. Advanced: Place two chairs back to back and about eighteen inches apart. Stand between chairs, placing hands on backs and supporting your weight on your arms. Keep legs straight; raise them slowly until parallel to floor and you are in sitting position. Hold position as long as possible, then lower your legs slowly. Rest for a moment. Repeat.

9

Take Pride in Your Neck Development

A strong, shapely, well-developed neck is a sign of bodily vigor, while a thin, or flabby, or generally underdeveloped neck reflects poor physical development.

Nothing sets off the body more than a powerful neck between a broad pair of shoulders. The influence of a well-developed neck on the posture is gratifying. It creates erect posture, squares the shoulders, and makes the back flat. In addition, your energy is increased vigorously, making your muscles dynamic in action and your body throb with the zest of super health and strength.

To the experienced physical director, the neck is a veritable index of health and power. It is perhaps the most vital link in the anatomical chain that influences our body condition. The neck's external musculature and its concealed muscles house the windpipe, esophagus, carotid arteries, jugular vein, vocal cords, and the thyroid and parathyroid glands. The spinal column protects the most important nerve trunks we have, which branch throughout the body and connect with the brain to regulate all our physical actions, forces and organic functions.

Unfortunately, most courses or systems of exercise tend to ignore the neck completely, or else throw in a neck exercise or two as an afterthought. This is inexcusable, since many body builders are therefore inclined to neglect these vital muscles, which are not difficult to improve or develop. Of course, the neck receives a certain benefit from the overlapping effects of other bodybuilding movements, such as overhead exercises or lifts, or activities such as wrestling, hand balancing, roman ring work, etc.

Resistance exercises, in which the muscles of one part of the body are pitted against those of another part, are well adapted to increasing the size and strength of the back, front, and sides of the neck. Repeat these exercises, which should be sufficient for the average person, from ten to fifteen times each, in the order described. As certain of the neck muscles are subject to strain, the beginner should take care to work up the resistance in these movements very gradually. Perform all the motions smoothly, without the slightest jerk. See the following pages for the exercises.

Exercises of this nature should be practiced to perfection before weights are employed. Starting this way, you will avoid the unpleasant kinks one gets from advanced exercises 5 and 6 on page 67.

Further advanced exercises allow the lifting of heavier weights.

1. Stand erect. Rotate neck in full slow circle. Reverse direction after each circle.

2. To the left: With hands grasping back of head, fingers interlaced, pull head forward to chest, resisting meanwhile with neck. Return head backward against the pressure of hands. Repeat. Make both motions as complete as possible.

3. To the left: Press palms against forehead. Force head forward and downward. Push head backward against resistance of throat muscles. Repeat. Depress corners of mouth for additional development of throat muscles. Excellent exercise if your neck is flabby or wrinkled.

4. Place right hand against right side of head. Push head to the left, toward shoulder, against resistance of neck. Return head to the right shoulder against pressure of right hand. Repeat for left side (pressing left hand against left side of head, and so on).

5. The best weight-training method for developing front part of neck necessitates employment of head strap specially designed for the purpose. (Purchase such a strap or make your own.) Adopt position shown. Body movement is confined to head and neck alone—rest of body is held rigid. Lower head backward as far as possible without strap slipping off. Raise head as far forward as you can.

6. The exercise best employed for development of muscles of back of neck. Adopt position shown. Keep body motionless—apart from head and neck—and lower head forward as far as you can. Then, move head backward as far as possible.

Variation: Turn head from side to side. Follow through by rotating head in complete circular movement.

NOTE: Do not bend over too far. Maintain a well-balanced position to avoid neck kinks, and place your hands on your thighs as a means of control. Gradually work up to ten reps per exercise with two to three sets.

10

You Must Stretch and Limber Your Muscles

Stretching is perhaps the most natural form of exercise. Watch a cat or dog, or any zoo animal. Regardless of what other exercise an animal may get, stretching is one habit practiced many times a day. If the human animal would think more about stretching and thus free his and her muscles, there would be fewer sprains and strains to contend with.

Stretching may be one of the few natural instincts that remain with the human family. Whether you are young or old, strong or weak, that natural desire to yawn, followed by the desire to extend your arms while expanding your chest, will be the manifestation of your body's need to escape from muscular idleness. This instinctive movement usually follows a period of inactivity or sleep, or when your body has been held in a cramped position too long.

The moment you expand or reach out any part of the body when that natural impulse demands, you are relieving undue tension, discomfort, restriction, and stiffness in the blood vessels, nerves, and muscles. Many times you are unaware of this constitutional benefit. Thus the body is promoting its own well-being.

Now that we recognize stretching as a valuable form of bodily movement, we can extend that instinct into a few moments of voluntary expression with various types of exercises, and as a result intensify the benefits to the body. Because of its wonderful loosening effects on all the body articulations, stretching can be termed "freeing movement." It is the type of activity that allows for a strong contraction of certain muscles followed by a complete relaxation. It allows the muscles to be kept at their normal length. For this reason, stretching exercises should always supplement developing movements, especially in the weight-training programs of those individuals who wish to obtain a more complete and vigorous development of the body.

When you stretch; carry each movement to the fullest extent possible without straining. All the movements should be performed slowly and deliberately. Follow each stretch by completely relaxing. This feature distinguishes stretching from other exercises.

There are many stretching exercises of great value for special needs. You will find it natural and easy to develop those yourself as you learn how stretching loosens up the muscles and helps to tone up the system by increasing and improving circulation.

Stretching exercises are of as much benefit to those who are too slender as to those who are too stout. Office workers who are at their desks all day will welcome this simple method of relaxing tired muscles.

One simple yet very effective exercise requires no effort on your part. Just place a chinning bar as high as possible in a doorway and hang from it, letting the weight of your body stretch your spine. If you are too tall to try this in the average doorway, you can achieve the same effect by bending your legs back at the knees so your feet clear the floor.

When doing this exercise, count slowly up to 60 to get a full minute's s-t-r-e-t-c-h. You can stretch your chest and arm muscles also by extending your arms across a doorway and letting your body sway forward.

The inversion, or upside-down, posture position—your standing position in reverse, with feet up, head down—relieves all parts of the body from discomfort, restriction, and stiffness. Special apparatus on the market today will allow you to gradually adjust to the full extended upside-down position.

The following exercises are just a few of the many movements you can perform. Stretch whenever you feel like it. You do not have to conform to any set discipline. But above all, make a habit of it. Repeat the exercises within your capabilities. Breathe in deeply when extending the limbs or body. Exhale fully when relaxing the movement. Vary the stretching exercises in your morning and evening practice sessions.

Remember—an erect, graceful and energetic body radiates health and youthfulness!

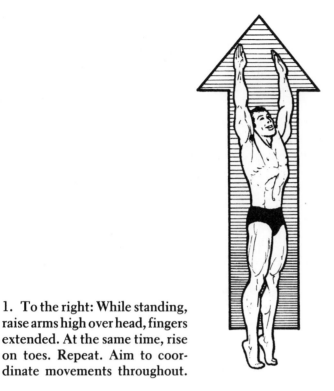

1. To the right: While standing, raise arms high over head, fingers extended. At the same time, rise on toes. Repeat. Aim to coordinate movements throughout.

2. To the right: Stand, hands clasped behind head. Turn whole trunk from hips to right. Bring it back to position, then turn it fully to left.

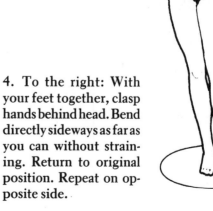

3. Stand erect. Stretch arms to their full length overhead. Bend forward, reaching down as far as you can with both hands. Return to original position. On next downward movement, swing arms to left of left leg. Return and alternate to right leg.

4. To the right: With your feet together, clasp hands behind head. Bend directly sideways as far as you can without straining. Return to original position. Repeat on opposite side.

5. Place one foot on a table or other support about the height of your hip. Then bend forward and touch your head to your raised knee. Repeat with other leg.

6. To the right: Stand erect. Stretch arms directly forward to full length overhead. At same time raise right knee upward as high as you can while maintaining balance. Pause and return to starting position. Repeat with left leg.

7. Sit erect on edge of chair with light wand or broomstick behind neck and across elbows. This compels arms to remain well back and in line with trunk. Twist to right as far as you can without straining. Return to original position. Twist to left.

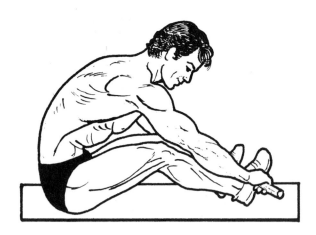

8. To the left: To stretch spine, arms, and leg, place a bar across instep as shown. Draw knees close to body and then begin to push out by straightening legs. Resist leg pressure by pulling back with hands. When performed properly, arms, legs, and back will feel the pressure.

9. Without moving your back or shoulders, move your neck from right to left. Backward and forward. Rotate it.

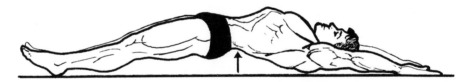

10. From a reclining position, stretch upward with arms behind head. At same time, arch back and stretch downward with toes. Twist and turn limbs and body in various positions so that all muscles get thorough stretch.

11

Advanced and Special Weight-Training Routines

After you have trained faithfully for a few months, you will have laid a good foundation for a strong, healthy, well-proportioned body.

If any part of your body appears to lack balance, ignore it until you have completed your entire training program, to give the underdeveloped part a chance to respond. If the problem part fails to respond satisfactorily to your complete program, you can begin to consider exercise specialization to bring the underdeveloped muscles up to par and make your body perfectly symmetrical.

The following systems of specialization have helped a lot of bodybuilders. In order for you to get the best results out of any of these special training methods, you must commit yourself to a thirty-day training program.

Further information about advanced training routines can be found in the various fitness-muscle magazines.

The Set System

The set system is a vigorous training routine that allows no rest for the muscles.

First, select four exercises for the part of the body you feel needs work. You are going to practice each exercise in sets—in other words, you are going to repeat the exercise a certain number of times, lowering the amount each time.

For example, say that you decide on a set order of 9-8-4-2 (which is, by the way, a good order to start with). Starting with your first exercise, perform it nine times, then eight times, then four times, then twice, pausing a few seconds between each set of repetitions to rest. Go on to your second exercise, and perform that one in the same manner.

Follow this program for two weeks. After the second week, increase the number of repetitions in your sets, practicing each exercise using the order 10-9-7-4-2.

The order of sets changes according to the muscles involved in the exercise. You cannot go far wrong. The larger muscles, such as the legs, the back, and the biceps can be exercised more vigorously, but do not use a greater set program than 12-10-7-5-2-2. Smaller muscle groups can use a set order of 6-4-2-2.

Every movement must be a determined effort. You can rest a few seconds between each exercise, but do not take prolonged rests. The muscles function better when they are warmed up.

The Repeat System

This thirty-day training method is also divided into segments of two weeks each.

Select four exercises for the muscles you wish to concentrate on, using plenty of weight with each exercise. Ordinarily, with weights, use no fewer than six reps per exercise and no more than nine. After you have completed the four exercises, take a slight rest and then repeat them in the same order as you did before.

For the first two weeks, repeat the four exercises no fewer than six times and no more than nine. After the two-week period is up, select four other exercises for the parts of the body you are specializing on and practice them every night, as before. However, the last two weeks of exercise should be much stiffer. You should increase both the number of repetitions per exercise and also the amount of weight used in each exercise.

The Strength Step-Up Method

This method of specialization is purely for increasing your strength. This is also a thirty-day training program divided into two-week parts. First, select four to six weight exercises for the muscles you wish to strengthen. Each exercise you perform twelve times, performing the first four repetitions with whatever weight you select. For the next four counts, increase the weight by five pounds and the last four counts by another five pounds.

The next two weeks, perform the first three repetitions with whatever weight you select to begin with. Increase the second three counts with seven and one-half pounds; the third three counts with another seven and one-half pounds, and the last three repetitions with another seven and one-half pounds.

The weight increases given here are the minimum you should consider. If you are specializing on your leg or back muscles, the increase can be greater. In some exercises, such as those for the abdomen, triceps, or neck, where less weight is usually used, the increases should be less. This is for you to determine according to your ability. Don't strain yourself, but do go all out and make your muscles creak with downright honest-to-goodness effort!

The Bulk, or Weight-Increasing, Method

With this method, you concentrate all your exercise on the largest muscle groups in your body: the back, chest, and thighs. An inch of muscle gained on these areas adds pounds, whereas an inch elsewhere only adds ounces.

Select twelve exercises from your courses, four for each muscle area. Practice every day as each course advises, selecting one of the first three special training methods explained herein.

Circuit Training

The purpose of this method is to develop overall fitness and body conditioning. It involves the overload principle, which uses a greater number of repetitions, lighter weights, fewer sets, and practically no rest between exercises to place more stress on your muscles. No matter how much weight you use in this system of training, the movements should always be performed in a constant, steady fashion without taking time to rest. If you can't get through the program without resting or straining, you're probably using too much weight. It is best for the beginner to select a given number of exercises for each body part, performing one set with each body part as you alternate in sequence. As your endurance improves, you can perform three to six workouts with one set, before advancing on to two sets. Six workouts with two sets will usually be required before moving on to three sets. How much you increase your overload intensity will depend on your particular needs and time limitation. To ensure the needed intensity of circuit training, you can: increase the resistance or weight used; increase the number of repetitions; increase the number of sets; decrease your rest time between sets; practice twelve to sixteen exercises as outlined in Chapters 6 and 7, alternating upper-body and lower-body exercises; keep a personal record or chart listing exercises with the repetitions and sets performed; and train three times a week.

12

Try Olympic Weight Lifting for Greater Strength and Power

Aside from fitness, shape, and muscular beauty, the most valuable gains to be derived from lifting weights are strength and power. There is little distinction to be drawn between weight training and weight lifting. Both involve the lifting of barbells and dumbbells, and when weight is gradually added to the bar, the result is increased development and strength. The differences between weight training and weight lifting are in the overall objectives. The weight lifter perfects his or her lifting ability in order to increase strength so that a heavier weight may be lifted, whereas the bodybuilder or weight trainer may have any of a number of objectives, among them increased strength, endurance, power, and flexibility. These are essential for any athlete.

Every bodybuilder should decide at the outset just what result is desired from his or her training, then plan or regulate the training accordingly. If, for example, you want to attain your maximum lifting ability, it is imperative that you train all parts of your body to work in concert. Otherwise, regardless of how strong your individual muscles may be, you will never be able to utilize the sum total of your physical power. The ideal workout routine should embrace both barbell exercising and weight lifting proper—whether your objective be muscular development or lifting ability.

Even though you may not have the slightest desire to become an Olympic lifter, the principal value of these coordinated movements will build muscle, strength, and all-around physical ability.

At present, only two of the three original Olympic lifts are being practiced: The snatch and the clean and jerk. However, the military press, now ruled out of competition, should be practiced in all training programs, since this lift, properly and strictly performed, will build strength and power. Of course, you should condition yourself with many months of bodybuilding exercises and intelligent training before attempting any heavy lifting.

Therefore, practice the three Olympic lifts as an exercise routine along with your other workout routines. Since these lifts involve learned techniques and skills, intelligent and consistent application must be followed in order to perfect these skills. Just as the *power lifts*—the squat, bench press, and deadlift—are part of your progressive barbell routines, so should the Olympic lifts be practiced as bodybuilding exercises. In this way you are providing a new or increased resistance to comply with the growing demands of your improved physical efficiency and increased strength. In due time, you will understand and realize that to attain any degree of proficiency in handling heavy poundage requires much training, and that weight lifting is a skilled specialty requiring a great deal of speed and power, as well as strength.

The illustrations in this chapter will give you an idea of the style and the sequence of positions for the squat and clean and jerk lifts. Use just a bar or a weight light enough that it will not prevent you from performing and learning every detail of the technique. When you have perfected your style in the various lifts, you will be prepared to gradually work with heavier weights.

If your goal is to enter competitive lifting, get a good instructor or an experienced lifter to work with you. Expert coaching will help to eliminate the mistakes and faults. Study the styles and training methods of the champions. Get in touch with your local AAU office. Request their official rules book with descriptions of the performance of the Olympic lifts.

Olympic Lifting Terminology and Description

The Clean: Stand with your feet about shoulder-width apart, directly under the bar. Bend down with a movement at the knees and grasp the barbell. The grip is also shoulder-width apart; with the palms of the hands facing down. Make any slight adjustment in the width of the grip if a feeling of better balance is achieved. In one continuous movement, while keeping the back straight and the head up, lift the barbell from the floor or platform to the top of the chest. In this position the barbell should be resting on top of the chest in line with the shoulders.

In order to accomplish this, it is sometimes necessary to go into a "split" or "squat" position so as to get under the barbell. If your knee were to touch the platform, the lift would be disqualified.

NOTE: The clean is the basic component of all three lifts, but it is not a complete lift by itself.

The Military Press: After the clean, the weight is pushed above the head with the arms fully outstretched. Only the arms and shoulders can be used to push the weight above the head.

NOTE: This position must be held for two seconds for the lift to be considered successful, as must be the positions for the other lifts.

The Clean and Jerk: After the clean, the weight is jerked overhead by using any means of boosting from the legs and back as well as the pushing power from the arms and shoulders. This lift can handle the greatest poundage.

Two-Hand Snatch: This lift is the fastest lift of the three. It demands accurate timing in all sequences that govern the lift. Keep in mind that the weight must be lifted from the floor to overhead in one nonstop movement. With one terrific effort of your arms, back, and shoulders, pull the weight off the floor, keeping it close to your body, and with full coordination of your leg drive onto your toes with the final arm pull. This unusual lift demands explosive power and speed, with good balance in either the split or squat style.

Good coaching is a must to learn the lifts properly for competitive training.

The following illustrations and their description in sequence will serve as a complete guide to properly perform the clean and jerk and the two-hand snatch with the squat style.

NOTE: In the split style, with one terrific effort of your arms, back, and shoulders, pull the weight off the floor close to your body, using full coordination of your leg drive, and then on to toes with the final arm pull—with the legs splitting, one to the front and one to the back—without the knees touching the floor. The lift is completed with the trunk, hips, arms, and weight overhead in near-perfect alignment, as the front foot is brought back first and the back foot is brought forward.

The Clean and Jerk. Courtesy York Barbell Co.

1

1B

2

3A

3B

4A   4B

4C

5

6A   6B

7A   7B

8

The Snatch. Courtesy York Barbell Co.

1   2

3

4

5A

5B

6A

6B

13

Measuring Your Muscles

One of the basic purposes of physical training or bodybuilding is to improve the development, shape, and proportions of your body. However, ignorance of what constitutes full muscular development causes many young bodybuilders to claim improbable or impossible measurements. In their desire to impress or show up favorably, they claim exaggerated or impossible measurements.

The serious bodybuilder often asks, "What muscular proportions can I get if I conscientiously practice?" Behind that question is the unspoken ambition to equal the physical measurements of his or her ideal. Unfortunately, the optimal proportions of the human figure vary with respect to individual structure and skeletal thickness, which determines whether you have a slender, a medium, or a stocky build.

No matter what your natural structure and body weight, your body's splendor will always dwell in its symmetry. Balance is the keynote to perfection in bodybuilding. Historically, the world's most outstanding physiques, like the greatest athletic performers, became outstanding because their bodies possessed great muscular balance in addition to development. They succeeded because they were taught to train properly, using sensible methods and equipment.

As we know, physique contests are not decided on the size of one or two predominant muscular groups. It is the balance of the whole that wins the prize. Yet today there are certain circles that worship muscular hugeness bordering on monstrosity.

Do not let the craze for huge biceps, pecs, or lats entice you into a false position that you may come to regret. Keep the theme of muscular balance foremost in your mind. Remember that every muscle in your body is a contributing factor to the body's general efficiency and beauty, as well as to its longevity. All the great physique stars of the past—up to some of today's greats—cultivated their splendid muscular physiques along superb classical lines while preserving strength and power.

When you begin your development program, take a complete set of your body measurements. Then keep careful track of the progress

Arm
flexed

Arm
flexed

Neck

Chest

Chest normal

Arm
straight

Arm
straight

Waist

Waist

Forearm

Hips

Hips

Wrist

Thigh

Thigh

Wrist

Knee

Knee

Calf

Calf

Ankle

Ankle

you are making. In this way, you'll be able to get a practical mental picture of yourself. If you recognize the importance of muscular balance, then training within the symmetrical pattern will give you a body you will be proud of—and one that everyone will admire.

Some years ago, David P. Willoughby, an American writer and world authority in the field of physical development and anthropometric statistics, projected the following methods for proper measurements:

Use steel tape; or if you use a cloth tape, make sure that it is accurate. Have someone else take your measurements if possible. If you are obliged to measure yourself, it will be helpful to stand before a mirror so that the position of the tape can be seen. Record the height and the girth measurements in inches and fractions thereof; the weight, to the nearest pound. Girth measurements should always be taken with the tape at right angles to the axis of the body or limb at the point of measurement. No slanting of the tape is permitted.

Height to be taken in bare feet, body erect, heels together. (Make yourself as "tall"; as possible while keeping your heels on the floor.)

Weight should be taken without clothes; where this is impractical, the weight of the clothes should be deducted.

Girth Measurements

Neck: at the smallest part, just above the Adam's apple; head erect.

Upper arm: (flexed), at the largest part (greatest prominence); arm raised to shoulder level, elbow firmly bent, muscles contracted.

Forearm: at the largest part; arm straight, fist clenched, wrist straight.

Waist: directly next to the base of the hand (between the bony knobs and the hand); hand open, fingers straight, hand in line with forearm.

Chest (normal): at the largest part immediately under the armpits, the tape crossing the shoulderblades in back and the nipples in front; body erect; head up, breathing quiet, muscles relaxed.

Waist: at the smallest part, usually just above the navel; body naturally erect, abdomen neither drawn in nor protruded.

Hips: at the largest part, where the hips are broadest from side to side, and the buttocks deepest from front to back; feet together.

Thigh: at the largest part, usually in the crease just below the buttocks; feet about six inches apart, thigh muscles relaxed.

Knee: across the middle of the kneecap; thigh muscles relaxed, but knees straight; weight distributed equally to both legs.

Calf: at the largest part; heels down and the weight supported equally on both feet.

Ankle: at the smallest part, about two inches above the bony knobs on the sides of ankle; both feet on floor, weight distributed equally to each.

Be sure to take measurements of both right and left arms and legs. All girth measurements of the fleshy (muscular) parts should be taken with the tape in gentle contact with the skin. If you are lean or muscular, take girth measurements of the bony parts (wrists, knees, ankles) also with the tape in gentle contact with the skin. If you are overweight, take the latter measurements (wrists, knees, ankles) with the tape drawn snugly.

The following tables should help you determine your own body's degree of symmetry.

Optimal Zone of Male Symmetry

Biceps should be 17 to 23 percent more than forearm
Biceps (average of both) should be 97 to 103 percent of calf
Forearms (average of both) should be 29 to 31 percent of chest
Biceps (average of both) should be 35 to 37 percent of chest
Neck should be 37 to 39½ percent of chest
Chest should be 30 to 37 percent more than waist
Chest should be 8 to 14 percent more than hips
Waist should be 73 to 77 percent of chest
Waist should be 81 to 85½ percent of hips
Thigh should be 58½ to 61½ percent of hips
Calf should be 65 to 68½ percent of thigh

Optimal Zone of Female Symmetry

Biceps should be 12 to 20 percent more than forearm
Biceps (average of both) should be 79 to 84 percent of calf
Forearms (average of both) should be 27½ to 29½ percent of chest
Biceps (average of both) should be 32 to 34½ percent of chest
Neck should be 37 to 39 percent of chest
Chest should be 24 to 32 percent more than waist
Bust should be 28 to 36 percent more than waist
Waist should be 76 to 80 percent of chest
Waist should be 67½ to 71½ percent of hips
Hips should be 6 to 12 percent more than bust
Thigh should be 57 to 60½ percent of hips
Calf should be 60 to 64 percent of thigh

In women, the chest measurements are to be taken above the level of the breast. The bust measurement is a separate measurement taken with the tape at the level of the greatest prominence of the breast. Otherwise, all measurements are taken the same way for men and women.

14

Accessories for Home Training

There are many different tools for physical fitness and development. In the following pages we will examine the most practical equipment for home use. These accessories are light, compact, and portable, requiring little space; they are excellent fitness items for a trip or vacation; and they will add variety and fun to your workouts.

The weight-training enthusiast or bodybuilder will find that this type of equipment, when intelligently applied, will greatly add to the muscular benefits of weight training. Because of the varied kinetics involved, accessory equipment can develop muscles, tendons, and ligaments from different and unusual angles, and can also tone, shape, firm, and build and strengthen isolated muscle groups.

Probably all of the world's greatest bodybuilders and champions of physical development have, at one time or another, combined accessory equipment with their weight training to speed up muscular development.

Bench Your Way to Muscles and Strength

The bench is the most popular and widely used appliance in weight training. Ask most athletes how much they can lift, and you will probably be told how much they can bench-press. It's the accepted standard by which most athletes measure their strength level.

There are many varieties of benches from the standpoints of price, design, and construction. Depending on these factors, benches can be used for general physical fitness, bodybuilding, power lifting, athletic improvement, and rehabilitation. If you want to use a bench in your exercise program, browse through physical-fitness magazines or visit various gyms and spas before making your choice. This will give you a better idea of the bench that is best for your needs.

For the following exercises, we will use the combination bench with removable upright or weight supports. This bench is designed to be adjustable to graduated angles of incline. As the angle of incline becomes greater, the difficulty or overload of the exercise resistance also increases.

Benches also are designed to accept various attachments for squats, leg extensions and curls, dips, biceps curls, etc. These benches will stabilize and isolate direct muscle movement.

The following routines and exercises can be performed with the flat or inclined bench. As a beginner, you should select a weight with which you can perform one set of eight to ten repetitions without strain. After the first two weeks, perform two sets of eight to ten reps and gradually increase to three sets of eight to ten reps. When you feel that you have attained perfection of performance in all your exercises, you may increase to three to five sets of 10 to 15 reps per exercise, with progressively graduated weight increases.

1. **Bench Press.** Lie flat on the bench with your feet flat on the floor. Take bar with your arms extended above your chest. Your hands should be slightly wider than shoulder width. Inhale as you lower the barbell to the chest and exhale as you extend the arms back to the starting position.

Training Suggestions: Use a wide grip to develop outer chest muscles. Use a close grip of eight to ten inches apart to build inner-chest muscle fibers.

Develops: chest, arms, shoulders, upper back.

2. **Stiff-Arm Pullover.** Lie flat on the bench with barbell above your chest and your arms fully extended. Keeping your arms straight, lower the bar to a horizontal position above your head. Bring the bar back to the original position.

Training Suggestions: On each backward movement with your arms, inhale deeply and spread your ribs to their utmost without straining. Breathe out deeply as your arms return to starting position.

Develops: chest, rib box, shoulders, upper back.

3. **Seated Press.** Above and to the right: Sit on the bench. Begin with the bar at chest height and your hands slightly wider than shoulder width. Push the bar directly over your head until your arms are fully extended. Return to the original position and repeat.

Involves: shoulders, upper arms, upper back.

4. **French Curl.** Lie flat on the bench with the barbell at your chest, and your hands ten to twelve inches apart. Press the barbell above your chest until your arms are completely extended. Keep your upper arms in an upright position and lower the barbell down behind your head. Return to original position and repeat.

Involves: arms, especially triceps and forearms.

5. **Bent-Arm Pullover.** Lie face up on the bench with your head slightly extended over the end. Begin with the barbell resting on your chest and your hands slightly wider than shoulder width. Inhale, lifting the barbell off your chest and move it back over your head, lowering the bar to the floor. Exhale as you return the bar to the starting position, remembering to keep your elbows bent at all times.

Involves: shoulders, chest, arms, and upper back.

6. Lateral Raise. Lie faceup on the bench. Hold a pair of dumbbells directly over your chest with your arms extended and the palms facing inward. Bend your arms slightly and lower the dumbbells in an arc to the sides. Return in the same arc to the starting position. Remember to keep your arms slightly bent throughout the exercise once you have begun.

Involves: shoulders and chest.

7. Inclined Press with Dumbbell. Lie on an inclined bench holding a dumbbell in each hand at the shoulder. From this position, press each dumbbell upward until your arms are fully extended, as shown.

Training Suggestions: This movement can be performed with a barbell. Follow the same procedure. As you progress in strength, you can perform many of your flat bench movements in the inclined position to increase the overload or resistance.

Involves: chest and shoulder muscles.

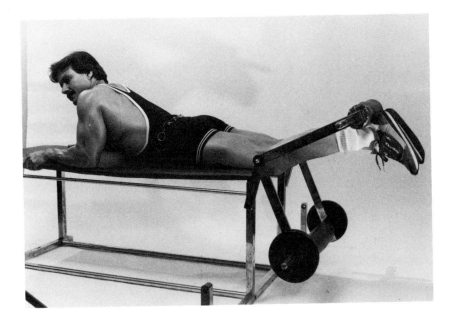

8. Leg Curl. Lie on your stomach with your legs extended under the top cushion bar. Curl the bar towards your back until the hamstring muscle is completely flexed. Lower slowly to starting position and repeat.

Training Suggestions: Leg Curls will mold the thigh biceps with clear-cut definition. The dual movements of extension and flexion will develop size, shape, and power in your legs.

Involves: hamstring muscle.

9. Front-Leg Extension. Sit with your legs behind the bottom cushion bar. From this position raise your legs until they are fully extended and the thigh is fully flexed. Lower slowly to starting position and repeat.

Training Suggestions: This extension movement will build powerful front thigh muscles and will strengthen knee muscles to prevent and rehabilitate knee problems.

Involves: thigh muscles.

Shape Up, Slim Up, Trim Your Waistline with the Slant Board

The slant board, also called an inclined board, abdominal board, or exercise board, is excellent for sit-ups, trunk twisting, leg lifts, and varied leg and arm exercises. Just lying supine on the board relaxes muscles and reduces the flow of blood to the feet.

There are various types of slant boards. The most popular for home use is the folding type, for easy handling and storage. The floor-ladder type allows the board to be adjusted to several heights, progressively increasing the resistance involved.

The use of the slant board to ease the gravity pull on the internal organs may seem to be of little or no importance, but don't let the feeling of tranquil inactivity fool you. Lying inert in a head-down position is one of the most relaxing and therapeutically effective exercises you can do. This comfortable exercise is performed by securing your feet under the straps and lying on the board with your head down and your arms either under the back of your head or alongside your body. There is nothing more to it—just relax for about fifteen minutes.

Sit-Ups

Sit-ups are the most common exercises performed on the slant board. They strengthen the abdominal muscles, hips, and thighs.

Secure your feet under the straps and bend your knees (this is always best for abdominal development—straight-legged sit-ups are not complete abdominal developers and affect the hip flexors). Place your hands behind your head, then sit up into your knees as far as possible. Lower to starting position and immediately repeat.

A variation on the sit-up consists of the same basic exercise with this difference: As you sit up, twist at the waist and touch the right elbow to the left knee. Return to starting position and repeat by touching the left elbow to the right knee.

Perform the movements smoothly and rhythmically. Take your time. Aim for perfection of performance. Allow your body to lie perfectly straight with your feet firm and your toes pointed. Exercise both sides equally. Exhale as you sit up and inhale as you return to the starting position. Try to perform each exercise at least six times, gradually working up to twenty reps. Do not exercise until two hours after eating.

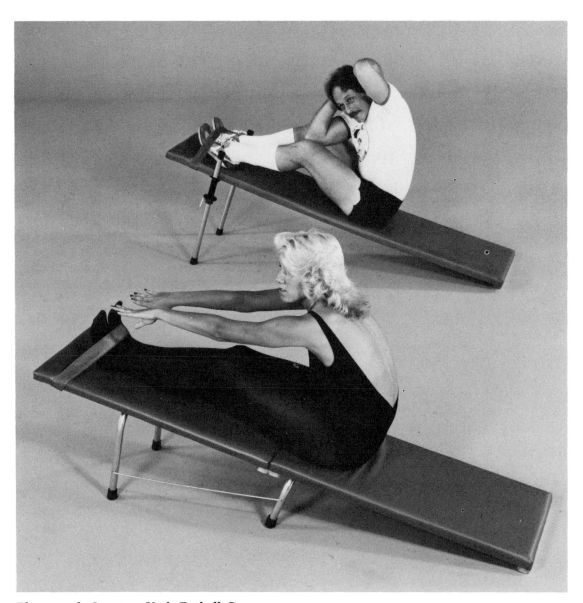

Photograph Courtesy York Barbell Co.

Starting Position: Assume prone exercising position. With feet placed firmly under leg straps at the high end of board, grasp handle bars (or straps) at a comfortable level. Breathe deeply.

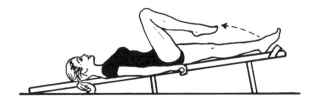

1. Bend right knee and raise leg to chest, flexing foot and pointing toes. Return to starting position and repeat with left leg. Good for reducing hips.

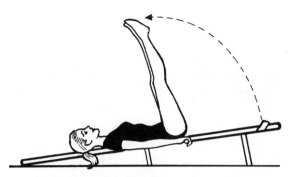

2. Press back flat against slant board. Keeping knee straight, raise one leg as high as is comfortable. Lower slowly and repeat with other leg. Advance to raising both legs at once and lowering together slowly. Flattens tummy bulge.

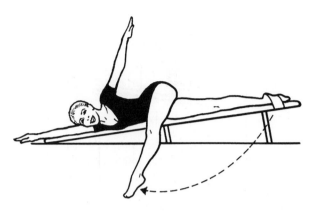

3. Lie on board on right side, right foot firmly placed under strap. Stretch left arm up and overhead. At the same time stretch left leg over and down, touching floor on right side of board. Turn and repeat on other side. Narrows hips and waist.

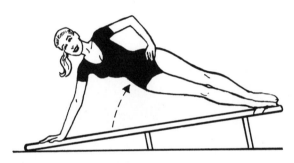

4. Place both feet under straps, one behind the other. Keeping body rigid, place right hand on right hip. Push up with left arm, raising body as high as possible, lower slowly. Reverse position to exercise right side of body.

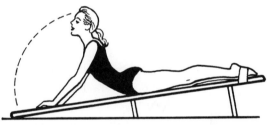

5. In same prone position, with feet placed firmly under strap, place hands on a table at shoulder level. Arch back, keeping hips on board, and raise shoulders, straightening arms as you do so. Lower body slowly and repeat.

6. Bend arms, placing elbows and forearms flat on board. Slowly raise up to a semisitting position. Return slowly to original position and repeat. Improves tone of waist and trunk muscles.

7. Raise arms over head. Keeping legs straight, bend at waist, lift body, and touch fingertips to toes. With arms still overhead, return slowly to starting position. Repeat several times and relax. Tones the waist and back muscles.

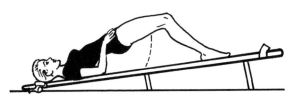

8. Bend the arms and place elbows firmly on table. Keeping shoulders on the board and feet in straps, raise hips slowly, using abdominal muscles to lift. Return slowly to starting position. Tones vital trunk muscles.

The Ever-Popular Chinning Bar

Whenever I have been asked to recommend a simple, inexpensive, and inconspicuous piece of bodybuilding equipment for installation in the home, my recommendation has always been a chinning bar. If you have one, then you know of the many interesting exercises and feats of strength and gymnastics that can be practiced on it.

There is nothing like a chinning bar for developing the upper body. The arms and shoulders are powerfully stimulated to muscular growth, greater strength, and endurance, as are the muscles of the chest and back. The gym bar presents an advancement in physical training that can be shared by everyone, particularly by those who find it inconvenient to use heavy weights in their homes.

Usually, the first thought that occurs to beginners on approaching a chinning bar is how many times they can chin themselves. With each chin, the entire body weight has to be lifted by the strength of the arms. In this feat, the lightweight person has a distinct advantage, and the heavyweight, even though he or she may have strong arms, often finds that the lighter-bodied athlete can beat him or her easily.

Ideal for Beginners

The common question asked by all beginners is, "How many times should I practice each exercise?" No set rule can be made because of the varying body weights and strengths of different people. You must make your own schedule, using as many repetitions per exercise as will enable you to perform a set number of exercises until you are just comfortably tired.

The person who has the most difficulty in chinning the bar is the heavy person, who has more body weight to lift. Today, the problem that made it difficult for the heavy and the weak to enjoy the thrill of chinning the bar is a thing of the past. The adjustable chinning bar has solved the problem. It is no longer a fixed overhead unit. By sitting on the floor and placing the adjustable bar between the door posts, an inch or so higher than the stretched arms overhead, anyone can practice the many interesting arm-chinning exercises.

When in the seated position, your heels should remain on the floor while you chin yourself, with your legs bearing a portion of your body weight. By pressing with your heels on the floor, you can regulate the amount of body weight to be lifted with each chin. This allows the weak-armed and/or heavy person to practice chinning-bar feats. Better still, this simplification enables you to create a chinning exercise routine that can build your arms, chest, and shoulders quickly.

It takes only a few weeks of chinning-bar practice in the seated position to equip you with the muscle and power that will enable you to perform the same routine from the full-body hanging position with the bar placed overhead. Of course, it is understood that you must practice all the seated chinning exercises on the progressive principle in order to develop the power.

You will find that the full-hang chinning movements are much more difficult to perform, since now you must lift your total body weight. Do as many repetitions as possible without straining. When you are able to perform fifteen to twenty reps, increase the resistance by adding or supporting more weight to or around your body. You can, for example, wear iron boots or a weight-supporting belt, which will allow you to comfortably add more weight as needed.

For greater muscular power and definition, perform at least three sets of each movement. If you are unable to perform the suggested reps, then do fewer reps but more sets. Put plenty of power behind each repetition; breathe deeply and regularly. Make your pull-up even and steady, without jerking your body; keep your arms completely flexed, almost touching the chest.

An excellent supplementary movement is simply hanging from the bar, arms outstretched, for a minute or two at a time. This exercise is great for stretching and loosening the shoulder joints and for stretching the muscles of the thorax and the spine, thus improving your posture.

If you are too tall for a full-length stretch in the doorway, place your feet well back, bending at the knees, so that your arms can come to full length when starting the movement.

Finally, check your bar frequently to make sure that it is *tightly engaged or locked into the wall,* to avoid injury.

The first five exercises that follow are to be done beginning in a seated position. The rest are from a standing position.

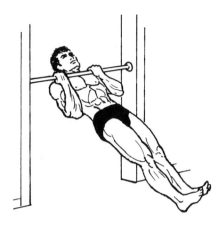

2. Reverse-Hands Grip. Perform this exercise in exactly the same manner as exercise 1, with the exception that in this exercise you grasp the bars with the palms of your hands facing your body. This exercise is easier, but it calls for stronger contraction of your biceps muscles. In order to give these muscles the strongest action, strive to pull yourself up until your chin is over the bar.

1. Natural-Hands Grip. Place the bar high enough so that you have to stretch your body to grasp it while seated on the floor. Grasp the bar with the palms of your hands turned to the front. From this position, using your arms only, pull your body up until your chin touches the bar. Keep your legs straight and allow the heels to rest on the floor throughout the exercise. Lower yourself slowly to the starting position and repeat.

3. Alternate Grip. Chin your body to the bar by grasping the bar with the palm of one hand facing toward you and the palm of the other hand facing away.

4. Wide Natural-Hands Grip/ Wide Reverse-Hands Grip. Grasp the bar with the natural-hands grip, but with your arms spread apart as far as is comfortably possible. From this position, slowly chin yourself to the bar. For the reverse grip (illustrated), grasp bar in reversed position, with your palms facing your body.

This exercise has a powerful influence on your back and shoulder muscles, as well as on your arm muscles.

5. The Neck Chin. Grasp the bar with a wide natural-hands grip. Pull yourself up until your neck (not your chin) touches the bar. Bend the head forward and under as your head approaches the bar. A good exercise for the deltoids and back muscles as well as arms.

Standing Chinning Exercises
1. Slow (or Endurance) Chin. Pull yourself up to chin the bar as slowly as possible from the full body-hang position, inhaling throughout. The slow chin can give you a good check on the improvement of your chinning power. Begin to count as you begin to chin, making a note of the number of counts it took you to chin the bar. The slower you chin, the longer you count. Keep a record of your counts.

2. **Pull-Up Behind Neck.** Grip the bar, palms facing front, with hands twelve to eighteen inches wider than shoulder width. Without any body swing, pull up until the back of your neck comes into contact with the bar; lower until the arms are completely straight, then pull up again. Good for the shoulders and upper back.

3. **One-Sided Pull-Up.** Commence as usual with the body hanging straight but with the hands about shoulder-width apart. Pull up to one side, then lower and pull up to the other side; repeat as many times as you can. Very effective in developing the upper-back muscles.

4. **One-Hand Wrist Chin.** Start with the main working arm straight, and pull your chin above the bar. Practice the movement often—using both arms equally, of course—giving the one arm less and less assistance, and you will eventually be able to perform one-arm chins unassisted, a really super feat. Perform at least three sets of each movement. If you can do only five repetitions, do more sets.

To the left: Hanging from the bar is good for stretching shoulder joints and thorax muscles.

To the right: The tall person may have to bend the lower legs backward.

Dynamic Bodybuilding Routines with the Chest/Cable Expander

The chest expander, consisting of rubber or steel-spring cables, has always been a popular exercising appliance. Just where and when it originated or was invented is somewhat vague. European athletes and strongmen date its use back two or three generations, and in the 1880s the fabulous Eugen Sandow used cables or strands to supplement his training programs. Later he advocated cable use in his physical-culture instructional teachings and campaigns.

Over the years this unique appliance has been used by professional and amateur alike. It is ideal for the beginner, and it is an excellent addition to the training program of the athlete, strongman, or advanced bodybuilder. Cables have also been used for remedial or curative exercises in hospitals and rehabilitation centers.

Perhaps the cables' portability has led to their widespread use. They may be comfortably carried about and conveniently used in even the most confined spaces. Cables are perfect for those who travel frequently.

Despite adaptability and diversification, cables are capable of testing the strongest athlete. The easy addition or subtraction of a cable makes it a unique appliance for progressive increased-resistance training. As you pull or stretch the cables along their range of motion, the resistance becomes greater—whereas weights maintain the same resistance throughout. Therefore one method complements the other for diversification in a good training program.

Before starting out on the program of cable bodybuilding presented in this section, be sure to read and understand the following instructions thoroughly.

- Look at the illustrations carefully. If possible, practice in front of a large mirror; this will help you to perfect your techniques and performance.

- Never strain yourself. Your object is to train and build your body. If the exercise repetitions are too much for you, cut them down. If they're not enough to tire you, increase them—gradually.

- Start with one cable for the first few days. This will limber you up and stretch lazy muscles.

- When you feel you have mastered the exercises correctly, add the second cable.

- Use the third cable only when you can perform all the exercises perfectly with the total repetitions as outlined.

- Follow the same procedure in sequence with additional cables.

- Practice six or eight exercises each day and vary them over a period of weeks until you have mastered all of them. Learn to select the number of cables for each exercise that will tire the muscles comfortably within the stated repetition count. Gradually increase the number of cables and movements per exercise.

- Exercise both sides of your body equally. Do as many exercises for the right side as you do for the left.

- *Take a firm grip on your handles. Never release your grip when the cables are stretched out or when holding the handle down with your foot. They may snap back and cause serious pain and injury. Hold Securely.*

- Never hold your breath. Breathe naturally at all times. If you find it difficult to breathe properly, then learn to breathe in as you pull or extend the cable, and exhale as you return to the starting position.

- You do not have to practice all the exercises at one time. Do some in the morning and some in the evening. Develop a schedule that fits your available time.

Strength-Training Routines

This type of program should be performed only after you have conditioned yourself through many months of training. The advanced training consists of a few exercises to tire the muscles within two to four repetitions by employing near-maximum resistance or poundage. This routine may be repeated several times at one training period, using few repetitions and high resistance in a series combining cable training with dumbbell and barbell routines.

1. The Body Lunge. Stand at attention, holding expander in front of thighs. Now lunge forward with one leg and at same time carry arms upward and backward to position shown. Return to starting position, alternating legs. Repeat at least eight times; work up to eighteen.

Benefits: Excellent for starting out each day. It will limber you up and stretch lazy muscles.

2. Extended Arm–Leg Lunge. Hold cable diagonally across back. One hand is by thigh, other at shoulder. Lunge forward and at same time thrust arm held at shoulder forward and upward. Repeat eight times with each arm; work up to eighteen.

Benefits: Starts to work on your arms and shoulders.

3. Pullover. Lie flat on floor with cables held across thighs. Now slowly, keeping arms straight and inhaling, stretch out expander to position behind head. Maintain stretched-out position for a moment, then return to starting position, slowly exhaling. Perform eight times, working up to twelve.

Benefits: Begins to work on building up your great lung and chest power.

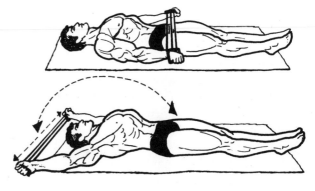

4. Knee Bend. Hold cables, arms straight above head. Pull down, stretching out to arms' length behind shoulders. Execute in conjunction with bending of knees. Return to starting position. Start with six counts, work up to eighteen. Inhale going down, exhale up.

Benefits: Calls for balance and coordination as it begins to limber you up.

5. Shoulder Joint Rotator. Hold expander across back at thighs. Stretch out and carry arms straight and upward over head, down to front of thighs. Return to first position in same manner. Do twelve times.

Benefits: A wonderful back, shoulder, and joint loosener as well as going to work on better posture development.

6. Arm and Kick-Up Coordinator. Position as in exercise 5. While bringing arms to overhead position, bring left leg up at same time to horizontal position. Perform eight times with each leg.

Benefits: Will start you on moving your arms and legs in well-timed coordination and is not as easy as it looks.

7. Sit-Up. Sit with arms extended straight out. Stretch cables back to shoulder, lowering upper body to floor. Return and repeat movement six times, working up to fifteen.

Benefits: Starts to work on abdomen, tightening up muscles around waist and stomach.

8. Neck Developer. Stand erect. Twist cables to gather them in middle. Hold expander in back of head at neck. Push cables out parallel in front and at same time work head back and forth against cables. Perform without straining eight to twelve times.

Benefits: Works on neck for improved appearance, better posture, and for more advanced work to come.

9. Shoulder Shrug. Place right foot firmly in handle. With arm slightly bent, pull with shoulder so it touches ear. Return to starting position. Repeat eight times; gradually work up to twelve. Repeat with left shoulder. Grip handle with palm facing up. Be sure foot is placed firmly in handle.

Benefits: The shoulder shrug, develops mainly the muscles of the shoulder region (deltoids).

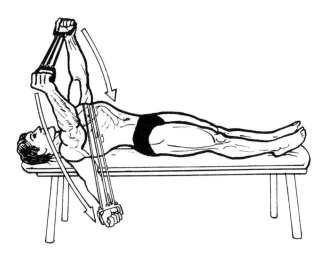

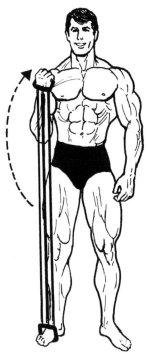

10. Bench-Lateral Raise. Lie down on narrow bench or box. Extend body straight out, with expander held straight above chest. Pull cables out sideways and downward to pass shoulder level as far as you can. Repeat twelve times. Progress gradually to eighteen times. Perform evenly and slowly throughout.

Benefits: Begins to develop and stretch upper portions of front chest (pectoralis major, front deltoids, and coraco brachialis). Also aids posture.

11. Front Arm Curl. Hold cables to the side with arm perfectly straight. Without bending back, bend arm at elbow, slowly bringing hand to shoulder. Return slowly to first position, repeating from eight to twelve times. Grasp handle with palm facing up. Be sure foot is firmly placed in handle.

Benefits: A terrific biceps developer.

12. One-Arm Press. Hold expander diagonally across back. One hand held firmly by your side, grasp handle with palm facing up. Now push bent arm directly upward to its fullest extension. Always maintain straight arm directly to side. Repeat at least eight times, working gradually to sixteen counts. Work other arm in same manner.

Benefits: Great for building up strength of triceps.

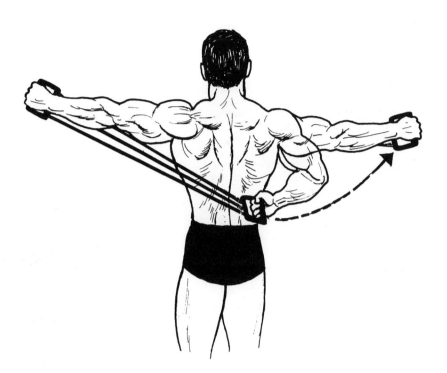

13. Half-Arm Extended Raise.
Above: Hold cables as shown. Pull out directly to extend position at shoulder level. Repeat eight to twelve times. Repeat with other arm.

Benefits: Excellent for wrist, shoulders, and other concealed muscles of forearm.

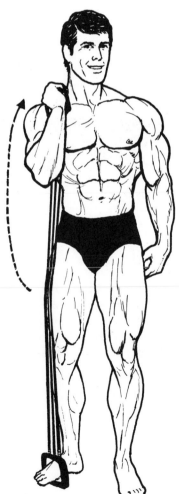

14. Reverse Curl. To the right: Put right foot in handle loop of expander and grasp other handle, palm down. Standing straight and without moving body, raise arm by twisting it so that hand is at shoulder. Repeat eight times. Then place left foot in handle and change to left hand. Try to do this twelve times with each hand.

Benefits: Great for upper-arm development, especially biceps muscles.

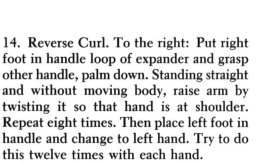

15. **Overhead Downward Pull.** Hold expander directly above head, palms facing each other. Pull outward slowly and evenly until cables reach directly across back on a level with shoulders. Return to first position, repeat for ten counts. Work up to sixteen repetitions.

Benefits: Excellent for upper-back and shoulder development.

16. **Foot-Arm Riser.** Hold expander with straight arms across back of thigh. Place toes on telephone book with heels on floor. Slowly pull cables outward and upward to position above your head, and at same time rise on your toes as high as you can without swaying. Return slowly to first position, pulling expander outward and downward to position across thighs. Repeat twelve times, gradually progress to twenty-four repetitions.

Benefits: Loosens up your back, shoulders and leg muscles.

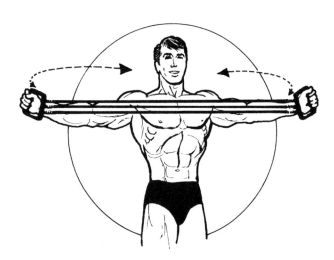

17. **Front Chest Pull.** Hold cables at arm's-length in front of body, and while taking a good, deep breath, draw each hand evenly and steadily until they are in a direct line with the shoulders. Repeat eight to twelve times.

Benefits: For upper-chest and lung development.

18. Side Arm Raise. Grasp handle firmly with foot and straight arm. While keeping arm perfectly straight, raise sideways to shoulder level. Return slowly and repeat eight times with each arm. Also vary this movement by performing it directly to the front.

Benefits: Great shoulder developer.

19. Back Lateral Raise. With straight arms, hold cables in back of body, palms of hands facing each other. Slowly pull outward and sideways to level of your shoulders. Return slowly, repeating eight times. Gradually work up to twelve counts.

Benefits: Tremendous for triceps, shoulder, and back muscles.

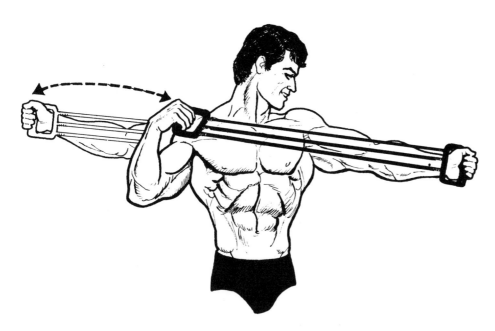

20. The Archer. Hold one arm directly sideways in line with shoulder level and the other bent directly to chest, but also in line with shoulder. Now slowly extend and draw out bent arm to its fullest extent in line with shoulder, ten times with each arm.

Benefits: When you pay strict attention to form, this movement is great for chest, back, and arm power.

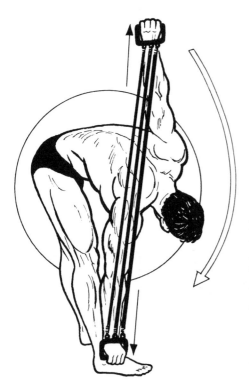

21. The Side Bend. With your cables held directly across back, push out to full arm's-length. Swing your right arm down to right foot and at same time bring left arm over in straight line, with your eyes following upward movement of arm. Return to starting position and repeat ten to fifteen times to each side.

Benefits: Excellent for hips, waist, abdomen, and lower back.

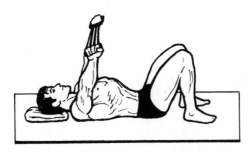 

22. The Neck Bridge. Lie on floor with expander directly above chest, knees bent, feet on floor. Now, while pulling cables down toward chest, lift hips off floor to bridge position, pressing on head and feet. Repeat twelve to sixteen times.

Benefits: Excellent for the entire neck musculature.

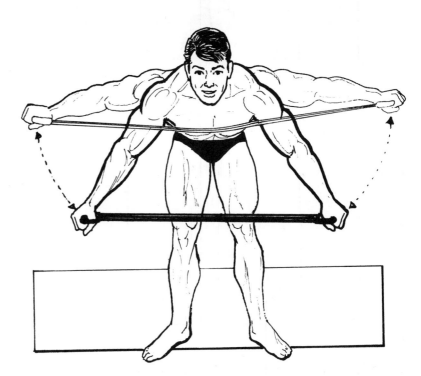

23. Bent-Over Lateral Raise. Stand with expander in position shown. Bring arms to chest slowly and return to starting position slowly. Repeat twelve times. Keep back straight by bending from waist only.

Benefits: Really gives upper-body and shoulder muscles a good workout.

24. The Great Abdominal Builder. Hold expander in front of body. Pull out to shoulder level and, while pulling, lower upper body slowly to floor, touching it with head. Return, allowing cables to help pull you back to starting position. Repeat eight times. Work gradually up to sixteen counts. (Place feet securely under something heavy for support.) Do not strain.

Benefits: Great for developing the muscles of the abdomen, stomach, waist, and hips.

Build Super Forearms with Handgrips and Other Equipment

Balanced development of the entire arm—from shoulder to fingertips—should be the objective of every bodybuilder and physique enthusiast. Unfortunately many bodybuilders, because of misinformation or a lack of training knowledge, fail to utilize correct training procedures for developing a strong, well-balanced, muscular arm. We see many enthusiasts with large upper-arm measurements who have underdeveloped forearms, wrists, and hands. This muscular deficiency usually stems from incorrect training.

Without getting into too much technical jargon concerning the principal muscles of the arm and their functions, suffice it to say that in the forearm there are twenty-two muscles, and eighteen in the hand. They are interrelated in action, and are capable of producing simple or complex movements. For example, opening and closing the hand by extension and flexion of the fingers and thumb is chiefly accomplished by muscles in the forearm coordinated with several groups of small muscles in the hand.

Usually, the forearm, wrist, and grip are the first to give out in any feat of strength requiring the combined action of all the muscles. Practicing the various exercises shown here will soon increase the strength and development of these weak points. You will no longer be limited by a weak grip.

Supplemental exercises and appliances for forearm, wrist, and finger development can be worked into your regular weight-training routines. Constant practice and intelligently applied training will reward you with a viselike grip and powerful forearms.

The ever-popular handgrips are used by athletes, strongmen, bodybuilders—in fact, by anyone who wants to develop a strong, powerful grip. Grips come in a variety of strengths and tensions—light, medium, and extra-heavy resistance.

The handgrip with springs is completely adjustable for everyone, however strong. Start with a resistance that you can handle easily; then gradually increase the tension of the springs as your power develops.

Study the illustrations and instructions at the end of this section carefully. Do not strain. Used consistently with your weight-training workouts, the grips will help produce a marked increase in the size and strength of your forearms, wrists, and hands. Bodybuilders and other athletes will certainly appreciate the results obtained from these exercises.

The power-weight gripping apparatus is a great supplementary piece of equipment that can be used in the gym or at home. The bodybuilder or strength enthusiast, in the quest for great forearm and gripping power, will find this apparatus quite beneficial. You can progressively increase the weight to meet the demands of your increasing strength.

One idea is to thicken or wrap your dumbbell and barbell bars where you place your grip. This increase in diameter makes it more difficult to handle the weight and, as a result, creates far greater stress on the

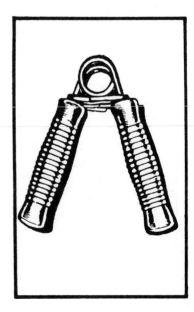

Regular handgrip.

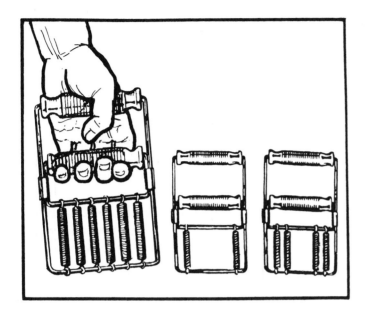

Adjustable handgrip.

Power-weight gripping apparatus.

Finger push-ups.

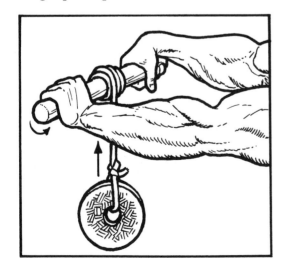

Wrist rolls.

forearms, wrists, and hands, which adds to building potential.

You must constantly strive to handle more and more weight in each exercise, thus building strength in the muscles, tendons, and ligaments with each session.

One of the fascinating features of grip building is the great diversity of exercises and stunts you can devise. Gymnast apparatus work is, of course, most valuable in cultivating a powerful grip. Using the horizontal or high bar, parallel bars, and rings, and climbing a rope hand-over-hand are some of the most effective methods for developing your grip. Push-ups, gradually removing one finger at a time, are also tremendous for strength and development.

Other exercises for developing greater strength and toughness in the fingers and wrists have been the favorites of champions the world over. To develop your forearms, take a newspaper and grasp one end with one hand, holding it at arm's length in front of you. Try to roll the paper into a ball by slowly manipulating it with your fingers. Do not cheat—try to accomplish this work solely with your fingers. You will find that this is an excellent finger, wrist, and forearm developer. You can also take magazines and newspapers, double them up, and try to tear them in half. This is fine work for the same muscles.

The wrist roller is a tremendous exercising appliance for the forearms, wrists, and gripping muscles. Bore a hole through the center of a wooden roller. Run a strong, four-foot cord through the hole, tying several knots in one end to prevent slipping. On the other end of the cord, attach a small weight or dumbbell—three to six pounds to start with. Gradually add more weight.

Stand erect, with your arms extended directly in front, palms down. Roll the rope around the stick until it is wound completely around the roller. Then reverse your hands and assume a palms-up position and repeat. Wind in each position two or three times.

The iron horseshoe provides many excellent possibilities for arm exercise. Various angles and positions of leverage movements can be employed while working out with this unique apparatus. Every movement is symbolic of some feat of strength.

Learn various movements that will give a twisting and turning action to your arms. Dip on your fingers instead of your palms, and try to do away with one finger at a time. This type of exercise will give your forearms and wrists ample work to develop that viselike grip.

Following is a series of exercises using the handgrips.

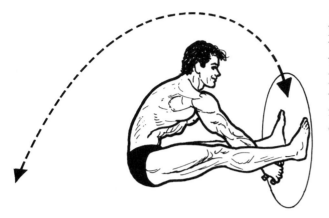

1. Stand erect, grips in hands, arms held high overhead. Stretch as high as possible, squeezing the grips, take a deep breath, and bend forward as illustrated. Release your tension on grips, exhale, return to original position. Start with eight repetitions and add one every third workout until fifteen are reached.

2. Stand erect, arms overhead. Squeeze the handgrips and bend from side to side, first the left, then right, moving only at the waist. Perform ten bends to each side, adding one each workout until twenty are reached. Keep arms stiff, move slowly and smoothly, inhaling when starting the exercise. Exhale when returning to original position.

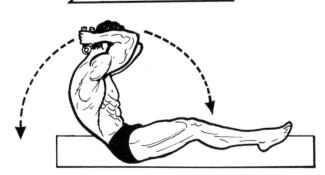

3. Lie flat on floor, legs stiff, toes pointed, arms bent at elbows, holding the grips at your head. Slowly raise your body, squeezing grips and keeping your legs stiff, and try to touch your head to your knees. Return to original position, releasing tension on grips. Start with eight repetitions, add one every third workout until fifteen are reached.

4. Lie flat on floor, keeping legs stiff and toes pointed, grips in hands at sides. While squeezing grips, slowly raise legs upward. Slowly and carefully lower legs to the floor while releasing tension on grips. Start with eight repetitions and add one every third workout until fifteen are reached.

5. To the left: Stand erect, with arms overhead, feet about twelve inches apart. Lunge forward with left leg, bending from waist and squeezing grips. Return to original position. Start with eight repetitions, adding one every third workout until fifteen are reached.

6. Stand erect, arms in front at shoulder level. Squeeze grips and squat down as low as possible to position as shown. Release tension on grips and return to standing position. Start with ten repetitions; add one every third workout until fifteen are reached.

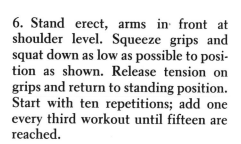

Increase Upper-Body Power with the Adjustable Crusher

The adjustable crusher body developer will provide novelty and diversion in your training. Its resistance can be increased or decreased to match the strength of any enthusiast. Muscles respond readily to this form of training because of its concentrated action. Employ as many springs with repetitions as your strength will permit. In movements where one arm is exercised, be sure to repeat an equal number of repetitions with the opposite arm.

You need not do the exercises in the sequence given. To save time, you can group together the exercises that use the same movements. Add springs as your strength increases. Oil the moving parts of the apparatus occasionally to keep in good working order.

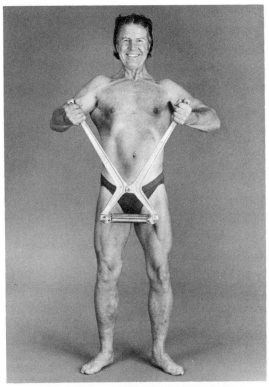

1. Hold apparatus at chest height; push handles together until your stopping point. Repeat. Good for pectoral muscles.

2. Hold exerciser as shown. Complete movement by crushing exerciser together, maintaining straight arms for best results. Good for chest, shoulders, and back.

 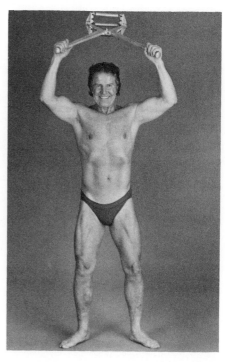

3. Hold exerciser as illustrated and complete the movement. This movement is more difficult when performed with straight arms than with arms slightly bent, but results are satisfactory either way. Develops upper chest and upper back muscles.

4. Assume position shown. Draw arms together as much as possible. The latissimus and chest muscles are greatly activated. Fine back developer.

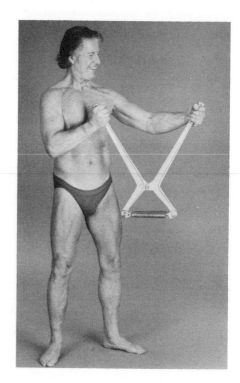

5. Place apparatus in position illustrated. Push handle of crusher down toward your body. Repeat with other arm. Develops upper arm muscles.

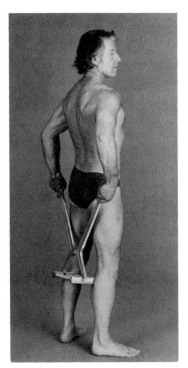

6. Hold exerciser straight out at arm's-length; bring hands together. Good upper-body builder. Perhaps one of the most difficult movements in this course.

7. Assume position shown. Push together exerciser handles. Keep arms fairly straight. Fine exercise for upper back and arms when properly performed.

8. Squat into position shown or sit on low bench. Place apparatus just above knee and bring legs together. Do not help with your arms—allow your legs to do the work. Aids leg muscles.

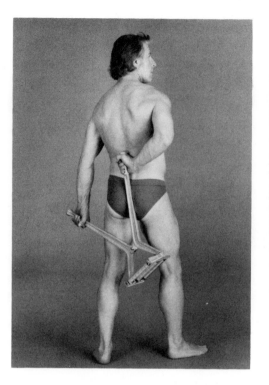 

9. Grip exerciser in manner shown. Brace apparatus against left leg. Press right handle toward left. Repeat with left arm. Aids triceps.

10. Another fine curling exercise done with both hands, employing maximum resistance. If crusher handles hurt sternum, wrap towel around handle for protection. Continue until arms are thoroughly exercised. Develops arm muscles.

Build Super Shoulders with Kettle Bells

The big shoulder muscles, known as the deltoids, cap the peak of the upper arms with a rounded mound of powerful muscle. When fully developed, they give added beauty to a well-developed arm and provide a striking and beautiful appearance to the upper body. These muscles aid considerably in developing full shoulder breadth. Without complete deltoid or shoulder development, no bodybuilder can claim complete development.

The exercises, when carefully followed through, will give excellent results when intelligently applied.

The revolving kettle bells are designed to be combined with the dumbbell. Simply insert the dumbbell bar through both openings in the kettle bell handles. Then load the ends of the bar and lock in place with the collars. This arrangement can help you to protect your deltoids

2. Raise bells to arm's-length overhead. Gradually lower one arm sideways to position shown. As you return arm to overhead position, lower other arm. Keep alternating with each arm.

1. Stand erect with kettle bells at shoulder height. Grip kettle-bell handles with palms facing front, so weight of bells lies back across wrist. Inhale and slowly raise bells to arm's-length overhead. Exhale as you lower your back to shoulder height.

from extreme leverage stress. As you progress, more weight can be added comfortably to secure even better results.

Practice each exercise six times. For every third workout, add one repetition until twelve reps are performed for each exercise. Then load each bell up with three pounds more and start over with the original six reps.

Advanced bodybuilders can start with poundage that they can comfortably handle, and they can perform three or four sets during their workout.

DO NOT STRAIN. Beginners should handle about twelve and a half pounds for each bell to start with, following the above procedures with extreme care. Keep your hands flexed at the wrists, palms down.

Here, then, are the exercises.

3. With bells held arm's-length overhead, slowly lower both bells until your upper arms are on a line level with your shoulders and your forearm at the half-straight position shown with palms facing out. Return bells until arms are straight overhead. Inhale as you lower; exhale as you return to overhead position.

4. Hold kettle bells at your shoulders, inhale, gradually lower your arms to three-quarter straight-arm position shown. Pause, then return bells to shoulders, exhaling as you do.

5. Hold bells at arm's-length overhead. Without bending your arms, lower bells with palms facing down, hand flexed at wrist, until arms are in a line level with the shoulders as shown. Pause. Inhale as you lower your arms and exhale as you bring bells to shoulders and press back overhead to original position.

6. Hold bells overhead, palms facing each other. From this position, lower your arms to position shown. Keep shoulders well back and elbows always in a line level with the shoulders—as much as possible. Inhale as you lower and exhale as you return to the original position.

7. Hold bells overhead at arm's-length. Slowly lower them directly sideways to the position shown. Keep your shoulders well back and your arms level with your shoulders. Palms must face up—flexed on the wrist. Keep your body erect throughout. Return to the starting position.

8. Hold bells overhead at arm's-length with your palms facing front. Then slowly lower bells to three-quarter straight-arm position as shown. Keep your elbows close to your sides throughout. Inhale as you lower, and exhale as you raise bells to straight-arm position overhead without pausing at shoulders.

9. Hold arms in a line level with shoulders, with bells resting on your forearms as described in exercise 5. Bend your arms at elbows, describing a quarter circle with bells until they touch your chest. Keep your elbows high throughout movement. Breathe in as you do so and out as you slowly return bells to original position.

10. Assume same starting position as in previous exercise. Instead of bringing both bells to your chest, however, at the same time, alternate your arms, one coming to your chest as the other straightens out. Keep your elbows high and body erect.

11. Stand erect with bells held at arm's-length overhead. Gradually lower arms directly in front, bells no further apart than shoulder width, until in position shown. Keep hands bent back on wrist and palms facing front. Breathe in as you lower and out as you return bells overhead. Keep arms straight at all times.

12. Hold bells in position shown. Raise one arm in a straight line with shoulder directly in front. As straight arm is lowered, begin to raise other arm, alternating the movement with each arm. Breathe in and out regularly.

Power-Twist Your Way to Strength

The dynamically diversified action of the power twister, when combined with intelligently applied weight training, will speed up results in developing your chest, shoulders, and back muscles, while strengthening your arms, wrist, and hands.

This type of supplemental equipment works your upper-body muscles at a different leverage range from that of weights. You will experience a continuously changing muscular action, enhancing muscular endurance.

This type of exercise variety helps prevent your training program from growing monotonous. For this reason your training workouts will become more enjoyable with this simple-to-use power twister muscle builder. Besides, it's light and compact and you can take it anywhere.

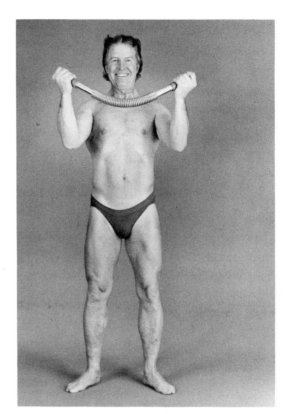

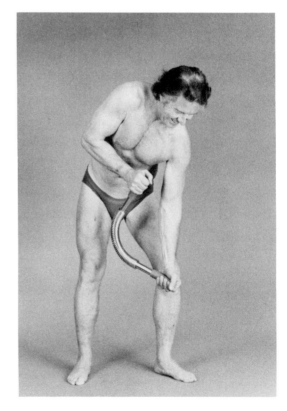

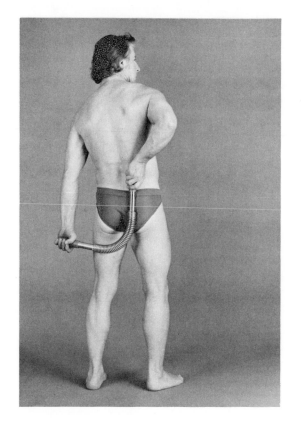
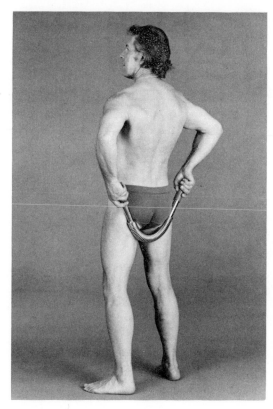

Study each exercise position carefully. Grip the twister firmly with your arms held straight as shown in the illustrations. Now bend or flex the twister with your arms and shoulders as illustrated, until your hands almost touch. Breathe in slowly as you bend the twister and out as you extend the twister slowly back to the starting position. Keep your body well braced. Do not strain.

Practice a few of the exercises, shown on page 132 to 134, at least six times each. Vary them from day to day.

As you become stronger you may add to the number of exercises performed. To create greater resistance, gradually extend your arms further from your body, increasing the stress. After you have mastered the movements, you can work them into set routines. You can devise other movements.

Be sure your hands are dry when using the power twister so that it does not slip. *Keep the handles away from your face while working out, in case your hands slip.*

The pictures were thought to sufficiently demonstrate what to do, so no captions have been supplied.

Iron-Boot Training
for Greater Leg Strength

Many bodybuilders today concentrate too much of their energy on developing their upper torsos, losing some of the powerful proportion and symmetry they could possess with intense leg workouts. If you're one of these bodybuilders, the following exercises were designed especially for you.

Just as dumbbells allow you to perform a variety of exercises for your arms, shoulders, and back, the iron boots make it possible for you to perform a variety of leg movements that will prove to be of great benefit toward building powerful, muscular legs and developing the hips and buttocks. This type of leg work should supplement your general weight-training activities—the squat, knee bends, etc.—rounding out your leg-training routines.

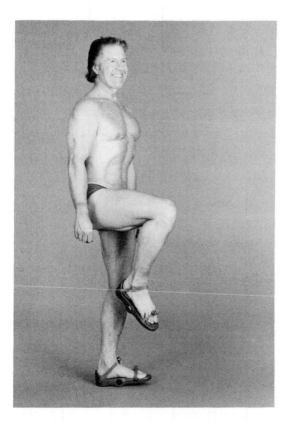

1. Stand erect. Raise right knee as high as possible to chest. Lower slowly to starting position and repeat. After twelve counts, repeat with left leg.

2. Stand erect. Raise right leg forward, as high as possible. Keep the leg as straight as possible throughout movement. Lower slowly and repeat. Perform the same way with left leg.

 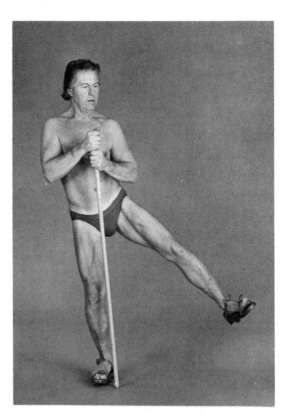

3. Stand erect. Bend right lower leg backward, as high off the floor as possible, with knee pointed toward floor. Return slowly to starting position. Repeat with left leg.

4. Stand erect. Raise right leg directly sideways and as high as possible. Return slowly to starting position and repeat. Repeat with left leg. Do not use or twist your upper body while doing leg movements.

The most popular shoes are made of aluminum or iron. The aluminum set weighs about four pounds, an ideal resistance for women to start with. The iron boot sets usually weigh about ten pounds and, with poundage added, will provide all the resistance needed by the strongest athlete.

The exercises must be performed carefully. This means no cheating. If you cannot perform the exercise with perfect balance, you are not prepared for the advanced leg movements.

At first, use your boots alone, or use sufficient weight to enable you to perform twelve correct movements and follow out the instructions accordingly. Every third practice session, add one repetition until eighteen counts are reached; then add two or three pounds to the boots and start over again from the original count of twelve.

Advancement consists in adding weight to the boots and duplicating the routine. For advanced training with weight increase, reduce the reps and gradually work your routine into two or three sets.

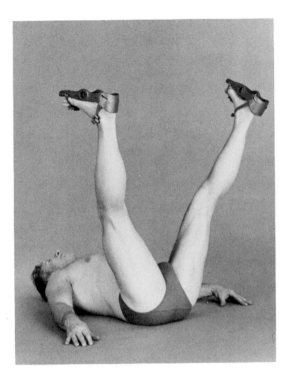

5. Lie flat on back. Raise legs to right-angle position. Keep them perfectly straight, and slowly part them sideways as far as possible. Pause, then bring legs back together at starting position and repeat. Excellent for muscles along side of thighs.

6. (The "bicycle" exercise.) Lie flat on back. Pull feet up overhead so body rests on shoulders and upper back. Support position with hands gripping hips and elbows maintaining this posture as illustrated. Lower one leg, and as the other begins to lower, push first leg upward and overhead. Continue revolving your legs in this manner as if riding a bicycle.

7. Lie face down, legs stretched out in straight line with your body. Bend lower legs to a right-angle position and toward hips as far as possible without straining. Lower and repeat.

At all times maintain good posture and balance; breathe naturally—never hold your breath.

Study the illustrations carefully. If you cannot perform twelve counts correctly, then practice until you are tired, and gradually work up to twelve counts. Thereafter, follow the instructions as previously described. You can achieve balance by using a rod, as shown.

Other Accessory Equipment

Many other home-exercising appliances can be purchased and used with great benefit in your fitness and exercise schedules.

The Multi Lift exerciser can be used as an all-around fitness, body and strength builder. It provides a progressive, graduated system of bodybuilding that is simple, safe, and sure for all abilities. It is perfect for those folks who don't have space for weight-training equipment.

Stationary bikes and treadmills, on which you can pedal or walk your way to better health without leaving home, are excellent for all members of the family.

Rowing machines come in many styles. The basic pull-and-push motion puts all the major muscles to work, providing excellent body conditioning.

Jump or skip ropes can provide a fast workout of benefit to the arms, legs, heart, and lungs. There are various types available, but it's best to invest in a good ball-bearing model.

Joggers and rebounders are aerobic indoor exercisers. They are designed to allow you to jog and run in the privacy of your home and are great for those folks who can't make time for outdoor jogging or for those who can't tolerate pounding the hard surfaces outdoors. There are many types on the market.

Bicycle trainer.

Multi Lift exerciser.

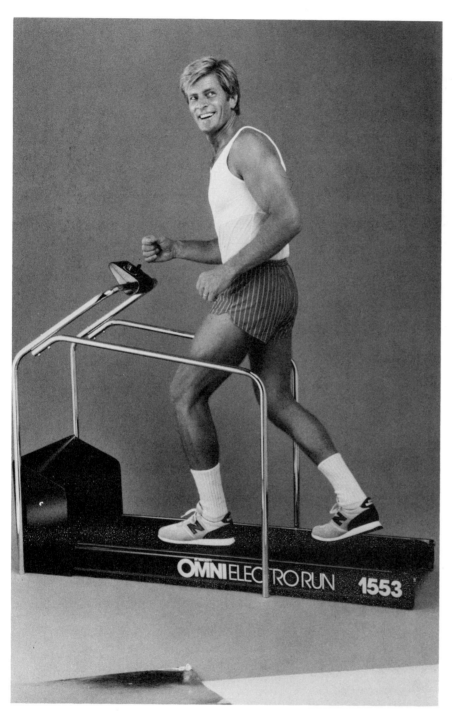

Motorized treadmill.

15

Massage Helps Muscles Grow

There is no longer any need to convince the average trainer of the fine results produced by using the assistance of massage to help bring the training of an athlete to a standard of efficiency and perfection. Unfortunately, most bodybuilders pay little or no attention to massage, and thus overlook a valuable ally.

Professionally performed massage is truly an art, requiring a good knowledge of the body muscles and their particular functions. The secret of massage lies in the manipulation of the muscles with the hands. While there are many different types of massage, in this case you only need to know the simplest form of manipulation, which you can do on yourself to advantage.

If you happen to have a companion sharing your bodybuilding sessions, each can take turns in massaging the other at the close of your training program. However, the muscles of your body that usually call for the most attention in bodybuilding are those of the arms and the legs. You can do the massaging on these body parts just as effectively yourself.

Most bodybuilders know from experience that the limb muscles are probably the most stubborn to respond to exercise treatment. The arm and leg muscles are used more constantly and vigorously than any other body muscles. This normally leads to a greater density of muscle tissue. The calf muscles are the most densely constructed, with the forearms a close second and the rest of the arm and leg muscles not far behind. Consequently, it takes more effort to break down this dense structure and make room for tissue replacement than is required by the more loosely structured muscles. Quite often, it seems impossible to get anywhere with the more densely muscled groups.

Apart from the active part massage plays in breaking down old muscular tissue to make place for new and greater growth, it injects a degree of pliancy into the muscles that keeps them tough and flexible. Massage prevents the appearance of knotty muscles, helping the growing muscles to form in their natural shapeliness.

I remember asking George F. Jowett, one of the pioneers in American bodybuilding, how he had developed his forearms and calves to such massive proportions with the hard daily working conditions he had to contend with. I was particularly interested in the development of his calves, which he increased from fourteen and one-half inches to eighteen and one-half inches. His answer: "Exercise and massage, with plenty of both in an orderly plan of training." In fact, massage is an important feature with many bodybuilders in stimulating the growth of muscles.

Many believe they should use massage only *after* they exercise. This is only partly right. It is equally important to massage stubborn muscles before you exercise. This loosens the muscle, improves circulation, and gets you off to a good start.

Massage is very simple: You just squeeze the muscle with one or both hands. Apply hand pressure so that the muscle is squeezed toward the center. Use gentle pressure to begin with; squeezing too hard can retard blood flow. Only after vigorous exercise should the massage be more vigorous, since more hand pressure is now needed to loosen the contracted muscular fibers.

After you have squeezed the muscles for a few seconds, take the muscles loosely between your thumb and fingers and shake quickly a few times. Follow this up with a brisk back-and-forth movement using the palms of your hand. This draws the blood to the surface. When treating the leg, always stroke up towards the body. The whole procedure should only take a few seconds.

A typical exercise and massage routine may go as follows: Select four exercises to be performed from eight to twelve times each, according to the nature of the exercise and the resistance used. Massage the muscles, then perform the first exercise. Afterward, sit down and repeat the massage. After a few seconds' rest, perform the second exercise, and massage after concluding the movement. Repeat the same process with the third exercise. At the conclusion of the fourth exercise, massage a little more vigorously. Rub the muscle surface a little longer and more briskly with the palm of your hand, to aid the circulation.

Wherever this method has been adopted, satisfactory results have been gained. But whether you are afflicted with stubborn muscles or not, muscular growth is always aided by incorporating massage as part of your bodybuilding program.

16

Choose Sports and Physical Activities for Health, Fitness, Recreation, and Pleasure

Every successful fitness and bodybuilding enthusiast or devotee should supplement his or her exercise routines with some form of enjoyable activity. Choosing one is simply a matter of analyzing your personal requirements.

There are so many ways of securing beneficial and pleasurable activity that everyone ought to be able to solve his or her problem of adaptability very readily. A little experimentation, seeking out proper instruction, and above all the real desire on your part are the keys. Some exercise methods and sports are described below to help you to decide which activities will suit you best. For more information, visit your local library or bookstore.

Aerobics: The aerobic system uses a regular, sustained regimen of exercises to improve fitness, endurance, and overall health. It is especially good for the heart, the cardiovascular system, the other organs, and the muscles. This system considers running, swimming, cycling, walking, running in place, and sports such as handball, basketball and squash the best exercise for attaining physical fitness.

Archery: This ancient sport can be practiced either outdoors or in a large hall, such as an armory. As you become more expert, competition can add to the sport's interest and fun. It principally uses the arm, upper-back, and shoulder muscles.

Auto-Resistance or Self-Resistance: This is a method of exercise in which one limb of the body offers resistance to another limb while a complete extension and flexion is repeatedly performed. Complete systems of this nature have been arranged by experts, and desirable results have been obtained. It is interesting to note that, in this system, an increase in strength does not require any increase in the number

143

gains. You can do the exercises very vigorously, or so lightly that they act more like a manual or manipulative treatment.

Apparatus Work: This not only greatly develops the arms and torso but gives you the ability to handle your own body with the grace and power of the accomplished gymnast. The transition from the novice stage to top-notch caliber requires perserverence and the utmost desire to succeed. Thorough leg work should be added to the apparatus specialist's program.

Boxing: Boxing can be very vigorous and taxing on the respiration. It builds confidence, coordination, and dexterity. Boxers should go in for some additional exercise that offers greater resistance to all the muscles.

Bag-Punching: This exercise is fun, develops the arms and shoulders somewhat, quickens the eye, and promotes accuracy. However, it should only be regarded as supplementary to a more complete exercise program.

Calisthenics: These are done to improve fitness and health. The nature of calisthenic movement has *everything* to do with the results obtained. A good, vigorous and thorough instructor directing the drill, plus plenty of ventilation, will produce excellent results.

Canoeing: This is a splendid outdoor sport, usually enjoyed in clean, inspiring surroundings. It can be extremely vigorous, or as mild as desired. Canoeing furnishes all the exercise you need for the arms, shoulders, and entire torso. If you combine it with mountain climbing or other vigorous leg work such as running or jumping you will have all the body developing work you need.

Dancing: Dancing is a splendid way to develop grace, suppleness, and health. Most people tend to underestimate the amount of strength and power needed for many types of dancing—for example, ballet dancers put in years of hard training in order to develop their muscles for the demands of the art. Those looking for less strenuous exercise combined with fun and relaxation can try ballroom dancing and disco.

Diving: While not especially strenuous, diving uses many parts of the body. Skill, coordination, and synchronization are the essential attainments in this sport. When combined with swimming and other water sports, acrobatic diving furnishes all the exercise needed for health and fitness.

Golf: The popularity of golf is a real testimony to its worth. It furnishes a form of moderate exercise that can be modified to meet all age requirements from eight to eighty. Many people spoil the sport's relaxation valve by becoming concerned and upset over their game; this counteracts much of the benefit. If you only play occasionally, you should be very careful not to overindulge. Once-a-week players should keep fit with other exercises.

Handball, Racquetball, Tennis: These exciting games bring every part of the body into play. There is no way (besides mountain climbing) of oxygenating the body more thoroughly. Do not expect any outstanding muscular development from these sports, and use them to augment a developing system.

Hiking: A daily two-mile hike is an excellent way to maintain general fitness, and can be especially pleasant and invigorating in a rural environment. The beginner should be careful not to overestimate his or her powers of endurance; comfortable footwear is essential. Hiking is a very enjoyable group activity, and a good way to find other enthusiasts is to contact your local hiking club.

Isometrics: This form of exercise involves pushing or pulling against an immoveable object in order to strengthen muscles. Sometimes isometrics can be beneficial to people who are confined to bed or otherwise restricted from activity.

Isometrics focus on specific voluntary muscles, and do little to stimulate the involuntary muscles, such as those of the heart and blood vessels. They also do not encourage overall flexibility and strength. Thus, isometrics are a supplement, not a substitute, for exercises that condition the entire body.

Isotonics: This term refers to all exercises that produce motion, as opposed to isometrics, which involve no movement. Isotonic exercises allow muscles either to shorten or lengthen over the full range of their motion. With movement, the mechanical efficiency of the body is improved, and the entire neuromuscular system is energized.

Most of the exercises detailed in this book are isotonic.

Jogging: Jogging is best defined as slow-paced running. The distance and speed vary among individuals, but they are closely related to the participants' age, sex, and level of fitness. Because jogging is informal and noncompetitive, it gives everyone an equal opportunity to get outdoors and enjoy activity, either individually or in a group. The intelligent application of jogging to your way of life can in due time lead to a greater sense of well-being and increase the capacity of your body to enjoy life to the fullest. Before getting seriously involved, investigate the necessary equipment needed, such as the proper footwear and clothing for different seasons. You should get a physical and OK from your physician before starting.

Mountain Climbing: "The outside of a mountain is the best thing for the inside of a man" is an excellent proverb. While you enjoy pure, clean mountain air and spectacular scenery, your legs, heart, and lungs get plenty of work. There is nothing like it!

Rowing: This is especially good exercise in a shell with a sliding seat, since the ordinary rowboat leaves the legs without sufficient exercise.

of movements, since your resistance automatically keeps pace with any Rowing of any sort uses the pulling muscles of the arms, back, and shoulders; therefore the rowing enthusiast should supplement with exercises entailing pushing with the arms. Leg exercise is also indicated if the boat seat does not slide.

Skating: Ice and roller skating offer top-notch exercise that uses the legs, hips, and lower back vigorously. Ice skating, especially on a cold, clear day, is second to no sport.

Skiing: Skiing is a splendid and vigorous sport. Propelling with the sticks uses the arms, shoulders, abdomen, and chest. The legs get plenty of work, especially going upgrade. No other exercise is needed when you get plenty of daily skiing.

Ski Jumping: This is the king of thrillers! The poise and skill of ski jumping, plus the strength required, puts it in the class of its own. It is, of course, only recommended for those hardy souls who have mastered every skiing technique.

Swimming: Swimming is a graceful and popular exercise that can also aid good muscle development. Professional swimmers build up an impressive amount of physical strength and stamina. The sport is often highly recommended for many people with disabilities that rule out other forms of exercise.

Team Sports: Popular team sports such as baseball, basketball, football, and hockey are great for health and enjoyment, depending upon the age and physical status of the participant. The amateur or outdoor enthusiast can derive much fun and healthful stimulation, provided the games are played away from dusty and smoke-filled playing areas. The once-a-week or vacation enthusiast should keep fit with daily exercises or routines as suggested throughout this book.

Tumbling: Tumbling on a suitable mat is one form of exercise that most devotees never tire of. It is best to have a good instructor since serious injury can result from a wrong move.

Wrestling: Wrestling is an excellent activity for developing a vigorous, muscular physique. No part of the anatomy is neglected. Wrestlers tend to retain their abilities longer than any other competitive athletes.

Walking: A great deal of good exercise can be had by leaving the car at home and walking anywhere from a couple of blocks to a mile or more. You can make these walks much more effective by walking correctly. Carry yourself well, breathe deeply, and reach forward with the hip as you take your stride. Put one foot in front of the other as though you were walking a six-inch plank; straighten your back leg fully at the end of the stride; slightly tense it for a second, and press well with the toes of that foot just before it leaves the ground.

Index